Standing Tall in Times Square

Herbert Murray

Inspiring Voices®

Inspiring Voices books may be ordered through booksellers or by contacting:

Inspiring Voices
1663 Liberty Drive
Bloomington, IN 47403
www.inspiringvoices.com
1 (866) 697-5313

ISBN: 978-1-4624-1093-4 (sc)
ISBN: 978-1-4624-1094-1 (e)

Library of Congress Control Number: 2014922421

Printed in the United States of America.

Inspiring Voices rev. date: 01/26/2015

Contents

"It is the character of growth that we should learn from pleasant and unpleasant experiences."

—Nelson Mandela
November 1997

The Nightmare

It all started on June 27, 1979, when approximately seven detectives banged on my door, guns drawn. When my common-law wife, Jackie, answered the door, they burst in, yelling, "Where is Herbert Murray?" When I came into the room, they grabbed me, threw me against the wall, put a gun to my head, and told me I was under arrest for murder. In the background, I could hear my thirteen-month-old daughter, Taneé, crying like crazy. Those detectives didn't have any regard for our lives—not my daughter's, Jackie's, or mine. It was the scariest thing I have ever experienced in my life. When I asked them what they were talking about, they told me to "Shut up."

I was taken to the Eighty-eighth Precinct, located on DeKalb and Classon Avenues. They took me to the interrogation room, where they questioned me about a murder that took place two weeks before on June 13, 1979. Can you imagine how confused I was? I was being charged for a murder I had no clue about. It seemed absolutely crazy. They were putting so much pressure on me that I couldn't even think.

I had to think about two Wednesdays ago. When the detectives asked me where I was on June 13, I told them I was with a housing police officer and four others: Vincent Brown, Ronnie Cook, Junior Washington, and Andrew Lambus. When I told him I was with a police officer, the detective left the room and came back about ten minutes later. He came over to me, smacked me in the face, and told me never to lie about a fellow police officer. That made me more confused. If I wasn't with the housing officer and the other four guys, then it had to be the other Wednesday when I went to the bank and withdrew $40 so that I could purchase a bike a friend was selling. The detectives didn't want to believe anything I had to say. The only thing they were concerned with was finding evidence to use against me when I went to court.

After they questioned me, they called in the assistant district attorney (ADA) to question me about the murder. I believe his name was Gallo. He gave me a little more information about what was going on. Gallo first asked me the same questions the detectives asked me. Then he asked me if I knew Joseph Hartman.

Wow, Joseph Hartman!

I knew him as Jo Jo. We grew up together. He knew my whole family, and I knew his. We went to public school together. Jo Jo was a little older than me; he was in the same age group as my brother. When I was sixteen, Jo Jo and I and four others were arrested for a small-time robbery on school grounds. The court gave each of us five years' probation. That crime took place in 1974 but played a big role in why I was being charged with murder. At that time, none of this made any sense. I was twenty-one years old, but mentally I may have been on a third-grade level. I couldn't read or write. I was so scared and confused I didn't know what to do.

ADA Gallo said Jo Jo supposedly claimed I was with him on the day of the murder. I told the ADA that if Jo Jo told him that, he was a liar. ADA Gallo was confusing me even more. I was sure he was trying to intimidate me so I would cooperate with him. He was trying to get me to incriminate myself, so he could use everything I said against me in court. He was a smooth guy. The only thing he was concerned with was getting a conviction when he took me in front of the judge.

As I mentioned before, I had to remember what I was doing two Wednesdays before. When I told ADA Gallo about the two stories, he tried to use it against me. He kept telling me I was lying, but I stuck to my story. Finally, he charged me with murder in the second degree. The detectives took me to central booking where I was fingerprinted.

They took my picture and did the paperwork so I could appear in court the next day. The detectives then took me to the Brooklyn House of Detention where I was locked up for a murder I did not commit.

As soon as I got the opportunity, I called my friend, the housing police officer. He told me no detective called him and verified I was with him and the others on June 13, 1979. I was furious!

Let me back up little. ADA Gallo told me this was a drug-related murder. Jo Jo and I were allegedly looking for drugs and ran into a guy named Marty, who was selling us drugs. I guess Marty said Jo Jo didn't have enough money, and Jo Jo told Marty he would be back. A half hour later, Jo Jo and I allegedly came back to buy the drugs. I later learned Jo Jo was hanging out with my brother that day. After the murder, someone identified Jo Jo at the scene of the crime. This witness said he knew Jo Jo and gave a description of the other person he saw with him that day.

But I had stopped hanging out with Jo Jo back in 1974 after we were arrested as teenagers.

My Upbringing

I grew up in one the roughest neighborhoods in New York City—Fort Greene, Brooklyn. My mother had seven boys and five girls. Hamilton was my mother's married name, and Murray was my mother's maiden name. Carolyn, Barbara, Debra, Michael, Anthony, and Jerome were Hamiltons. Calvin, Darlene, Steve, Cathy, Joseph, and I were Murrays. Everyone in the neighborhood knew my family, especially my brothers, because they were all fighters.

My mother was a very strong woman. To raise seven boys and five girls, she had to be. I remember my mother in the kitchen all day long. Everything was going, all the eyes on the stove burning and gospel music playing. She would be singing one minute and yelling at us the next. Everyone had to be home by the time the streetlights came on. If you weren't home by then, you wouldn't eat for the night. Yes, we all tried sneaking in the kitchen when we thought Mama was sleeping. Her room was right below the kitchen, and the floors were squeaky, so she heard everything that went on in there. She got out of her bed to enforce the no-kitchen rule, it was that important.

My mother didn't take mess from any of us. Everybody was scared of her, because she was a no-nonsense person. She didn't play games. She would pick up the closest thing to her and bust you in the head with it. I remember one day when I spoke back to Mama. I guess I was trying her because I thought I was grown. She picked up a broom and knocked me upside my head. That was the last time I spoke back to Mama in that tone. Mama was really hard on me, because she thought I was the slick one who got away with a lot.

My brother Steve and I looked so much alike growing up that Mama used to mistake him for me. Steve used to take my beatings, because I switched beds with him when I knew Mama was going to come after me when I did something wrong. Sure enough, Mama would try to sneak up those stairs. I always knew when she was coming, because I heard those squeaky stairs. I immediately hid in the bathroom. The next thing I heard was Steve crying, because Mama had beaten him instead of me. Steve and I laugh about that all the time now.

My mother was a beautiful woman and my role model. Even if she hadn't been my mother, I would have picked her as one by a long shot. She was both mother and father to me, and I learned a lot from her.

She taught all of us how to cook, iron, wash clothes, and clean. Cleaning wasn't just my sisters' chore. The boys cleaned whatever Mama told us to clean. We washed dishes, went to the Laundromat, and ironed our clothes for school. But the worst chore was picking up the welfare food. No one wanted to pick up that food because it was embarrassing. The whole neighborhood would know you were on welfare. But when it was time to pick up the food, we hooked the cart like we were going to the Laundromat. We really thought people didn't know we were going to pick up the welfare food.

Yes, Mama taught me well. I didn't understand it growing up. But I certainly understand her teachings now. She was a determined, hardworking, strong woman. I never saw Mama look weak or cry in any situation. She was something else. Mama saw I had that same strength, because I never gave up. I didn't get into the drugs so many guys my age were involved in at that time.

Heroin, aka "dope," had infested my community. People were going in and out of prison because they had to lie, cheat, or steal in order to take care of their habit. People were dying left and right because they had overdosed. People became homeless because they were strung out on heroin. I thank God that I was able to come out of the situation that

I saw trapping many black teenagers. I'm not saying I'd escaped entirely, because I was still affected by the community.

Still, I didn't have a sense of direction, and I definitely felt trapped. In fact, I remember trying to enlist in the US Army, but they rejected me because I had a criminal record. That was about two years after I was arrested with Jo Jo and those four other individuals. I recall the recruiting officers telling me that if I went back to the courts and tried to get my record expunged, he would allow me to join the army. But I never did go to ask the judge.

Some say that people don't become a product of their environment, but I'm a living witness to the truth of it. Our community had a high crime rate. Gangs ran the streets where I came from, and it was very poor neighborhood. I survived while many of those I grew up with are now gone, either dead or in prison. It's really amazing how many young black men waste their lives not knowing how to escape their environment.

The educational system didn't really help because the teachers were from the middle class. Their values were different from ours. They really didn't understand our situation of being poor. Yes, we were very emotional, angry, and hungry and felt really deprived. How in the world can a person who came from a different world understand what I was going through as a poor, young black man?

Maybe that was the reason why a teacher punched me in the chest. He just didn't understand why I was so angry. I didn't really understand why until I became an adult. So how in the world could someone else understand me? It's a very hurtful experience growing up in a poor family with a mother running the household on her own. Sometimes I sit and think about my past and reflect on the things Mama told me. Being kids, we were hardheaded. We thought we had all the answers, but we didn't know anything.

My father was never around. I really didn't know him. I remember one time when I played hooky from school and my mother saw me. I think I was in the sixth grade at that time. Anyway, Mama wanted my father to come over to kick my behind because she was getting older and weaker and wanted a man to discipline me.

Now, mind you, my father had never played a role in my life. He taught me nothing. I barely knew him. He was a total stranger to me. On this particular day after I got caught playing hooky, he came over. I don't exactly remember what kind of device he used—either a stick or belt—but yeah, he kicked my behind. I was so mad I ran out of the house. I was mad at the world. I was about ten years old, but my mind was like a six-year-old.

I rebelled so much that I got kicked out of public school when I was in the sixth grade. I remember my teacher, the principal, and my mother all got together and spoke about transferring me to an all boys' school. My mother gave them permission to tear my behind up when I got into trouble. After a while I started doing well at this school. My grades went up, and I became part of the basketball team; I went on field trips, and I felt the love from all my teachers. Most of the teachers were black, so there was a sense that they were more concerned about the kids as opposed to the public school I got kicked out of.

I did very well at this boys' school. I graduated there with honors. I went on to Eastern District High School. Most of my friends who graduated the year before me were at Eastern District. They were trying to get me to play hooky, smoke weed, and go to hooky parties. But I didn't want to get with that, because I wanted to play basketball. My mother was proud of me because I was doing so well in school.

Then my whole life came tumbling down when my mother died. All of a sudden I started hanging out with my former friends. I started playing hooky, I started smoking weed, I started going to the hooky parties. I didn't care about my grades. I didn't care about playing basketball. I really didn't even care about myself at that point.

My first encounter with the law was when I was arrested for fighting on the train. When the police came to break up the fight, the person I was fighting wanted to press charges against me. So I pressed charges against him too. We both went to jail. The judge let us out the next day. In fact, I wasn't even charged with a crime. I was charged with disorderly conduct, which was a violation. I think I had to pay a $100 fine.

Actually, on my arrest sheet, I only was charged with two crimes in my entire life. I'm not saying that is good, but I know individuals who have criminal records as long as my arm. In fact, Jo Jo was one of those individuals with a long rap sheet.

As a sixteen-year-old teenager in 1974, I saw a lot. I saw people from the Black Power movement as well as the lowest level of dope fiends. That's what happened to many of the people I grew up with. All of my brother Anthony's friends turned into junkies. The younger generations started messing with dope. That was the main reason why I stopped hanging out with Jo Jo, because he started messing with drugs. I appreciate my brother Anthony for intimidating me to keep me away from drugs.

I remember one incident when my brother Anthony saw me hanging out with Jo Jo. At this point, Jo Jo was a known cold-blooded junkie. My brother saw me with Jo Jo coming out of a building known to be a dope house. He thought we were getting high. My brother came over to me and smacked me so hard that he left his fingerprints on my face. My brother's assumptions were wrong, because although Jo Jo did shoot up that particular day, I definitely didn't. Jo Jo and Malik tried to convince me to try to use dope, but because of my brother's actions I didn't give into that peer pressure. So I definitely appreciate what my brother did.

By this time another person who was a great influence on my life had passed away: my big brother Mike. Mike was the man. He showed me mad love. He was my role model. He always gave me money. He made sure I was all right. I could even say that he was my father. Words can't describe how much influence he had over me. I don't think he even realized it. His death was really hard on me, even though I was something like sixteen years old when he passed. It was like people say, when death comes upon you, it comes in threes. My brother, my mother, and my grandmother all passed away within a three-year span. All these people who had a personal interest in me were dead. My life was a mess because at that point, I didn't have any sense of direction. I was uneducated. I was angry. I couldn't find my way. No one was around to guide me in the right direction. It took getting arrested with

Jo Jo and the rest of the individuals for someone to reach out and show me another way.

Ever since I can remember, I was a person who had a job. One of my first jobs was working for the egg man. I believe I was about ten years old. The egg man was the person who came around the neighborhood on a horse-drawn wagon selling eggs by the dozen. Everyone knew him because he was a good man. He gave all of our mothers credit. Some of the mothers didn't even pay him, but he still gave them credit. The egg man treated me like a son. I really don't know what happened to him. He probably has gone home to his higher power, because he was an old man when I was a kid. May God bless his soul.

I remember getting my working papers. I think I was thirteen years old. My first job as a teenager was working at an office. One of my responsibilities was to take boxes of lunch bags to the welfare center and give them out to those on welfare. I liked that because it gave me a sense of responsibility. This was a summer job, and every summer they sent me to a different work site. I remember having a job in a restaurant washing dishes or busing tables.

The restaurants were my favorite because back in those days they had agencies where you could buy a one-day job, a part-time job, or a full-time job in restaurants. Believe me, I had plenty of restaurant jobs between the time I was thirteen up until I got arrested for this crime. In fact, when I was arrested, I was working at this restaurant in the Village called The Other End. I started working at The Other End in 1974. I was sixteen years old at the time. I stayed on that job for five years up until I was arrested in 1979. When I started that job I was washing dishes and cleaning tables, and I gradually worked myself up to the position of a cook helper. One of my responsibilities was to open the place for business. I loved that job. It gave me a great sense of responsibility. My hours were from 11:00 a.m. to 7:00 p.m., with Tuesdays and Wednesdays off.

It seemed like everyone was shooting drugs in my neighborhood, so I decided to hang out in another neighborhood where I met some good brothers: Vincent, Rollin, Kenneth, Andrew, Bullock, and Big Junior.

They lived on South Portland Avenue and DeKalb Avenue. They were not too far from where I lived on Adelphi Street between Willoughby and Myrtle. I met them right after I stopped hanging out with Jo Jo. Although they were just a few years older than me, they had a better sense of trying to get themselves together as opposed to individuals like Jo Jo. We all looked out for each other like crazy. I mean, it didn't matter whether you had money or not. They showed love regardless.

Vincent and I were the tightest. Every time you saw Vincent, you saw me, and whenever you saw me, you saw him. We were like twins. His family accepted me as one of them. In fact, when my mother died, I was sixteen years old. I had to find a place to live because the house we were living in was up for sale. My father invited me to stay with him in Manhattan, but I didn't want to live with him. My brother Calvin went on to live in his own apartment. I didn't know at the time that my father had invited me and my brother to live in his apartment with his girlfriend.

I didn't want to live with my father for several reasons. The main one was that I didn't know him, and he didn't know me. When Vincent heard that my mother had died, he asked me to stay with him. He spoke to his mother, Ms. Barbara Brown (everyone called her Tuna). Ms. Tuna was like a second mom to me. She treated me like one of her own kids. She already had Vincent and Priscilla. She adopted me without any hesitation. Actually, she didn't officially adopt me. My oldest sister, Carolyn, became my legal guardian.

I stayed with Vincent's family for about a year until he got me a job working at The Other End in 1974. I got hired right after I came home from being incarcerated for the crime I did with Jo Jo, Michael, Willie, and Malik. I then rented a room for $25 a week on Dean Street between New York and Nostrand Avenues. Ms. Tuna was really proud of me because I was becoming a responsible young man. I stayed in that room for about two years.

Right after I started working at The Other End, I met the love of my life, Jacqueline McKnight. I met Jackie when I was living on South Portland with Vincent. I was kind of shy when I first saw her. I remember that day like it was yesterday because she was the most beautiful girl on South Portland. I met her through her brother, Johnny. Johnny was one of the boys on the block. Jackie and Johnny lived with their grandparents just a few doors down from Vincent's house.

When I first saw Jackie, Johnny and I were in his grandmother's backyard. Jackie and her friend Carol came in the backyard, and she immediately drew my attention. She had on a red blouse, white pants, and red shoes. That was a hot look. I was hooked. It was love at first sight. She was sixteen, and so was I. Johnny introduced us. I was sweating during the introduction.

I don't think her grandparents liked me because I was taking away their little girl who was basically taking care of them when I came on the scene. I remember her grandmother telling me to get out of her house and never to come back. However, that didn't deter us, because we fell madly in love with each other. Freddy, who was Jackie's grandfather, was mad cool. He used to have me fix his car and certain things around the house without giving me a dime. He used to always tell me not to tell Jackie's grandmother, because she would make him pay me to do those things. One thing I admired about Freddy was that he stayed sharp in terms of how he dressed.

I thought Rollin liked Jackie at one point so I didn't mess with her until Rollin went down south. I know that sounds like a coward move, but that was how we showed respect for each other. We didn't push up on a female when we knew one of our friends liked her. But boy, I made my move real fast because I wanted Jackie to be my girl by the time Rollin came back from down south.

I found out that Jackie never liked Rollin. In fact, she liked me, but she just acted like she didn't. As time went on, we fell in love. People were definitely trying to break us up. At one point, we stopped speaking to each other because of her grandmother.

Jackie really didn't hang out. She was one of those girls who went to school. She was going to Clara Barton High School, an all-girls school. Her grandparents became worried as we grew closer because I guess they wanted to protect her from a bum like me. You know how some parents can be: overprotective.

Jackie and I got our first apartment in 1976 on Prospect Avenue. We lived there for about eighteen months. When she became pregnant with my beautiful daughter, we decided to move to a bigger apartment. Vincent and his girl, Linda, lived on Woodruff Avenue in East Flatbush, in apartment 3D. There was an empty apartment right next door in 3B. He talked to his landlord, and the landlord gave us that apartment. It was very nice, with a big kitchen, wood floors, a huge living room, and affordable rent.

Jackie did a beautiful job fixing that place up. We went out and bought brand-new furniture for the apartment. Our living room set consisted of a couch and a love seat made of a type of velvet, and the end table was glass and chrome. The lamps were elegant. Jackie was definitely the organizer when it came to decorating the house. Of course, since we had wood floors, I did the floors. I used to have them looking like glass. You could have eaten off it, it was that clean.

I was into music. I remember we started out with a hi-fi system that my sister Barbara gave me. I got tired of that system and took out its speakers and made some new speaker boxes. But that sound didn't do it either. So I made another switch. I saved up enough money and put an amp on layaway. When I got the amp out the shop, I paid down on a really nice pair of speakers. When I finally got both speakers out of the shop, no one could tell me anything! My music sounded like a professional. As a matter of fact, I became a DJ—not a real professional, but a DJ nonetheless. I used to get paid for playing music for weddings and birthdays or just playing music at a spot.

I love me some music. Although I couldn't put my feeling into words how music affected me, I understand now what music does for the soul. It's a relaxer. Music helps you contemplate. Music helps you relieve pressure. Music makes you happy. I used have albums from wall to wall in my apartment. Every time I got paid, I used to at least buy two albums a week. I had crates of albums.

When my beautiful daughter was born, I was the happiest person alive. I tried to go inside the delivery room, but the nurse wouldn't let me. Every time I tried to go in, the nurse would tell me to go back to the waiting room. I really wanted to see the delivery because I used to hear a lot about fathers going into the delivery room and witnessing their child's birth. I don't know why they kept me from seeing my daughter being born into this world. I kept asking the nurse, and she kept telling me that was part of the hospital rules.

When I left that night after my daughter was born, I remember singing on my way to the train station. I was so happy because my baby girl was my first and only child. I'm not going to lie, I wanted a boy at first, but as long as God blessed us with a healthy girl, I'm more than happy to have a beautiful daughter. My whole life changed when my daughter was born, because I really became responsible not only for myself but also for an infant.

I still didn't stay home as much as I should have because I was still hanging out with my friends. I think hanging out with my friends was my biggest downfall with respect to being in a relationship. I fell short at being romantic. Not to say that I didn't handle my business regarding other aspects of the relationship. Yes, I was a provider. I was a protector, and I was a father. But I just fell short in taking Jackie out and being romantic, because I wanted to hang out with my friends. Remember, I was about twenty years old, but mentally I was probably on the level of a twelve-year-old. I couldn't read or write, and I did everything on an emotional basis because I wasn't a thinker.

It took Mo Junior, who was Vincent's cousin and the person I was with on the day of the crime, to give me a sense of direction. He encouraged me to stay strong and not to fall into the traps so many young people my age were falling into. Society placed crime, drugs, gangs, peer pressure, and the many other influences on us as young black men. Believe me, I ran with that advice and I haven't gotten into trouble since. It had been over five years since he gave me that advice.

But my past caught up with me. If I never had gotten arrested with Jo Jo and those individuals back in 1974, I wouldn't have anything to talk about in this book. During those five years on probation, I only got arrested one time for the train fight mentioned before. Other than that, I was a truly law-abiding citizen.

"I learned that courage was not the absence of fear, but the triumph over it. I felt fear myself more times than I can remember, but I hid it behind a mask of boldness. The brave is not he who does feel afraid, but he who conquers that fear."

—Nelson Mandela
1994

The Connection

I knew nothing about the murder until those detectives busted into my house to arrest me. When that assistant district attorney told me about Jo Jo's alleged involvement, I knew something was really wrong because I had stopped hanging out with Jo Jo many years before. But I also knew that, since that time, he was on drugs. When the ADA told me that someone had identified Jo Jo and me at the scene of the crime, I was so confused I didn't know what or how to think. I just knew I hadn't done anything, especially murder. Regardless, they arrested me and charged me with second-degree murder.

One of the detectives told me that if the State of New York had the death penalty, I would certainly be put to death. After they interrogated me, they transported me to the Brooklyn House of Detention on Atlantic Avenue so that I could appear in court the next morning. This was a holding facility for men. Most of the people there were from Brooklyn.

I arrived at night. The detectives took me to the receiving room where I was processed into the system. The first thing they told me to do was strip—completely. He took me through the process of spreading my butt cheeks, looking behind my ears, looking under my feet, rubbing my hands through my hair, and opening my mouth and rubbing my hands around my mouth. I really felt less than human. They took away the little self-respect I had by putting me through that process.

After they processed me, they escorted me to the sixth floor. It was dark, and there was a lot of noise coming from the cells. It was the scariest thing I had ever experienced, like going into a spooky house or something. As the CO (corrections officer) escorted me down the tier, the prisoners were looking at me from their cells as if I was fresh meat. The officer put me into a cell and slammed the gate so hard that it shook me. I sat there on the bed all night until it was time to go to court.

When the CO yelled "On the court," everyone who was scheduled for court that morning had to form a line to be escorted downstairs to the receiving room and divided by which court had called them. You had inmates going to courts in Manhattan, Brooklyn, Queens, and the Bronx, and the COs were yelling out names to get individuals onto buses to be transported to the courts.

I was going to the Brooklyn Criminal Court, which was right across the street from where they held me. We were escorted by the COs through a tunnel that was connected to the court. The receiving room was a madhouse because everyone was talking loud. Codefendants who'd been separated the night before now had a chance to talk before they appeared before the judge.

I had to wait all day to see the judge just to have my case postponed. According to the court officer, I had to be appointed a lawyer; therefore, the judge wouldn't see me. I was sent back to the Brooklyn House of Detention. My next court appointment was scheduled for the next day. When I got back from the court, I was so tired I could barely keep my eyes open. I didn't want to go to bed because I was afraid. The inmates were all in the dayroom playing cards, watching TV, playing chess or checkers, or just standing around talking to each other. There were probably around fifty inmates in the dayroom. I stood in the corner scared to death.

I was scoping out the area because I needed to get to a phone. I needed to find out what was going on with me. I had already spoken to my friend the housing officer the day before and he confirmed that I was with him and the others. I just wanted to speak to someone. When I finally got on the phone, the person who was running the phone told me that I had five minutes. I knew right then that it was going to be some mess up in here. When I'd barely started talking, this dude was saying I had only two minutes left on the phone. I was mad and I wanted to fight. But when my five minutes were up, I got off the phone.

Right after I got off the phone, I knew I was going to find a way to get more phone time somehow. There were about three guys running the phone, and each of them got at least an hour apiece. Mind you, you have some sixty inmates on my side of the facility. The guys running the phone looked out for their homeboys. They sold "clicks" (phone calls) for either money or cigarettes. You wouldn't believe how much some of these individuals were getting for a half hour on the phone!

In the facility there were individuals there who were charged with murder, but not nearly as many as the petty charges. There were also people who were in for political reasons. Those brothers stood out because they weren't down with the nonsense. They were always trying to educate those who were deaf, dumb, and blind. The others who weren't educated were trying to survive the best way they knew how.

Prison has the same mentality as those who are living in the street, and I was definitely familiar with street life, so I knew how to deal with those individuals. It was just a matter of becoming aware of the people who were in control or running things in there. One person I met when I came back from court was named Bernard. He was one of the guys who ran the phone. Bernard was a big dude, and I was kind of intimidated by him, but we clicked instantly.

It was almost time to be locked in our cells for the night. The CO yelled "On the lock-in," which meant that everyone had to go to their cell. When I got into the cell, I noticed how small it was. I could literally straighten my arms out and touch both walls of the cell. It had a bed, a sink, a desk that was attached to the wall, and a toilet. The cell wasn't equipped for an animal, let alone a human. I started crying because this was really scary.

I don't think I slept at all that night, because the next thing I knew the CO was yelling "On the chow," which meant that breakfast was about to be served. The same activities went on in that dayroom as the day before. People were arguing over food, and many felt that they weren't getting enough. It was a madhouse. When it was my turn to pick up food, I didn't say anything. I just accepted it and got out of the way.

As soon as I finished my food, the CO yelled "On the court." I went through the same procedure, waiting in the bullpen until the court clerk called my name so that I could go before the judge. When I got into the courtroom, all my witnesses were there. Vincent, Mo Junior, Junior, Andrew, and Ronnie were sitting right in the first row when I came into the courtroom.

First thing, I was appointed a lawyer, whose name was Joe Brensnader. The judge announced the charge I was accused of and asked me how did I plea to the murder charge. After I pled not guilty, the case was postponed to a month later. My lawyer then spoke to all of my witnesses and then came back to speak to me. He informed me that my witnesses supported my statement.

I didn't know what was going on at this point. I couldn't comprehend any of it. He informed me that I was charged with murder in the second degree, and the judge had denied me bail. He also told me that the case was going before the grand jury. He asked me what I was doing on June 13, 1979, at around one o'clock. I told him the same thing I'd told the ADA. He asked me to tell him what I did on that day from the time I woke up. I told him I went over Vincent's house who lived next door. When I got there, another friend of ours was there, Ronnie. We talked for a few minutes and then went over to Mo Junior's. Vincent's cousin Junior was also at Mo Junior's house when Vincent, Ronnie, and I arrived. We stayed there until Vincent went to work. Mo Junior volunteered to drive Vincent to work, so we all went with them.

When we got there, our boss, Dale Lind, a Lutheran pastor, saw all of us as we pulled up in front of The Other End. After we let Vincent out, Mo Junior drove us back to Brooklyn and he let Ronnie and me out on Fulton Street and Flatbush Avenue. I guess Mo Junior went home, but Ronnie and I went to the record shop. I bought two albums, and then we went to P.S. 20's park where we met Andrew. We all played basketball until about 6:00 p.m. We then headed to the liquor store and bought a pint of wine. We drank the wine and went our separate ways. I went home.

After I'd told my story to the lawyer, he told me that he would come and see me at the Brooklyn House of Detention. When I got back to the facility, the CO told me I had a visitor. It was Jackie. She'd been in the courtroom both times I appeared. When I got down to the visiting room, I had to be searched.

As soon as I got into the visiting room, Jackie came over to me, crying and asking me what was going on. I told her what little I knew. We talked about what happened at the house when those detectives busted in. We were both scared. It was like going blind or almost dying or like losing someone close to you. I could still hear my daughter crying and Jackie asking them what was happening, and the detectives telling her to keep her mouth shut in her own house. I remembered my face against the wall with three guns pointing at me. She was still afraid just talking about it while visiting me. The memories still come to me like it happened yesterday. I could repeat this story over and over, because I thought about that incident for many, many years. And I'm certain that Jackie will never forget that day either.

I never missed anyone as bad as I missed Jackie, although only two days had gone by. It felt like a very long time at that point. She needed me to sign my check so that she could pay the bills. As I mentioned before, I had gotten paid the day before they said I committed this murder. Unbelievable! The murder was committed on Wednesday, June 13, 1979, and I got paid on Tuesday, June 12, at approximately 8:30 p.m., so everything was closed. Back then there weren't any 24-hour check cashing places. I had to wait until the next day to cash my check. Thank goodness I had that check for Jackie, because she was going to school and wasn't working. My wages were the main income as far as the bills were concerned. I always asked myself, why would I want to rob someone when I had a check I hadn't even cashed yet? It made no sense.

Anyhow, it was about time for Jackie to leave the visiting room. She was only allowed to visit for an hour on certain days. If I remember correctly, I think my visiting days were Mondays, Wednesdays, and Saturdays. On alternate weeks there was a change to Tuesdays, Thursdays, and Sundays. The hour was coming to an end. I could see tears in Jackie's eyes. This was the first time we were ever separated, since we had been on our own. I could only imagine what was going through her mind. Our daughter was just thirteen months old. When it was time for her to leave, we hugged and kissed.

When I got back upstairs, I tried to get on the phone to call Vincent, but one of the phone guys told me I had to wait. I waited like two hours, and this same guy told me I might be dead as far as the phone was concerned. I was so mad that I wanted to fight. Bernard came over to me and told me not to worry because he had my back. I finally got on the phone around 9:00 p.m. Bernard told me to take my time because he didn't need the phone anymore that night.

I stayed on the phone about a half hour before he told me I had to hang up. The CO was about to call the lock-in when everyone had to go to their cells. If I recall correctly, lock-in was at 9:30 p.m. Everyone dreaded the time. No one wanted to be alone in their cell. There were many days that I felt like the walls were closing in on me, especially in the beginning. Those cells would drive you to suicide if you were weak-minded.

I still didn't know what was going on. Jo Jo was right across from me on the B side. He was claiming that he didn't know anything about the murder.

The CO finally called the lock-in. The only thing I could do in that cell was sit on that hard cot. I sat there for at least part of the night, thinking. All sorts of things went through my mind. But the main thing was I still didn't know a thing about my situation. I was thinking about Jackie. Even though I couldn't express my feelings about her at that point, I knew I was missing her. I guess loneliness was kicking in. I felt all alone—in a trap.

Tears started running down my face. Why was this happening to me? I was really angry. I was being charged with a murder I didn't commit. How can a person comprehend something like that? Everything I had ever done wrong in my entire life went through my mind. I really felt I must have done something terrible for this to happen to me. Why was God punishing me? I must have finally fallen asleep because the next thing I heard was the cell doors opening.

It was time for breakfast and for those who were scheduled for court to get ready. I been locked up for two days, and the only clothes I had were the clothes I was wearing. I hadn't taken a shower since my arrest. Jackie couldn't come to visit me until the next day to bring me clothes. I wasn't in a good mood at all. I didn't even eat breakfast. I just stood in the corner minding my business.

One of the telephone guys—in fact, it was the same phone guy who told me I was dead on the phone—came over to question me about my business. "Why are you in prison?" I looked at him as if he was a fool and told him if he didn't get out of my face, he going to have a problem. I don't remember my exact words, but I know they were definitely threatening.

Bernard came over and asked if everything was okay. I told him that I needed to get on the phone. He got me on the phone. I called Jackie and again, and we talked about what had happened. She started crying again because everything seemed so confusing. I told her I really needed clothes when she next came to visit me. She told me she wouldn't forget.

I knew Jackie for about five years. Can you believe that it was very difficult to have a conversation with her? Yes, we talked, but we never had an intelligent conversation because I wasn't on the level to have an intellectual discussion back then. Jackie was on that level because she graduated from high school. She knew much more than I knew. In fact, I remember her trying to teach me how to read and write, but I didn't have the patience, and I wanted to hang out with my friends. I was really ignorant.

When my phone time was up, Bernard tapped me on the shoulder and told me I had to get off the phone. I didn't have court that day. I only knew one person in the whole A side, Bernard, so I stood on the side where the phones were and watched everything. Those guys weren't acting like they were in jail. They were acting like they were in the park hanging out. The only thing that was going through my mind was that murder charge.

I went into the dayroom, where they were watching TV and playing games—card games, chess, and checkers. I really couldn't hear the TV because they were making so much noise, and the TV volume was up as high as it could go. I heard one guy yelling to stop talking so loud so he could hear the TV. Another guy yelled back and told him to shut up. The next thing I knew, those guys were fighting. I didn't even see it coming because it happened so fast. The next thing I saw were the COs running into the dayroom to break up the fight. These guys were fighting so hard, the CO who first came running into the dayroom couldn't break them apart.

One of the fighters was the guy who ran the phone. He was the one who got beat up. That didn't look good in my opinion, because in prison, only the strong survived. Even though I was in there only for two days, I knew what I had to do. I had to figure out how to get some control over the phone because I wasn't about to go to someone every five minutes to make a call. Bernard had a good reputation as far as controlling the phone. I also knew that I might have to fight for it too. I wanted to watch the news that was on TV, but you couldn't hear it. So, I stood in that corner watching everything until it was time to be locked in. Once again, when I got in my cell, I sat there nearly all night until I fell asleep.

When I got up the next day, I was in the dayroom in the corner again. One of the guys playing cards asked me if I wanted to be his partner in spades. I told him I didn't want to play cards. I wanted to get on the phone so I could call Jackie, but every time I tried, the guy who'd gotten his butt kicked yesterday kept telling me that I had to wait. I was getting upset because this punk was fronting. I said to myself that I was going to take his phone spot as soon as I got a little more familiar with the pecking order.

As I stood in the corner, I noticed a circle was forming around two individuals. I didn't know if they were about to fight, but I knew something was about to happen because everybody was watching and waiting. Then they started sparring. They said that no one could hit in the face, but they could hit as hard as they liked on each other's body. I guess the first one to quit would lose the challenge. Sparring was a method used to challenge someone you thought you could beat. If you wanted someone's sneakers— or anything else, for that matter—you asked him to challenge you for it.

THE COURTS

I was in the Atlantic Avenue facility for a month, and a whole lot happened in that time. When I appeared in court again, Jackie had brought me clothes. I had spoken to all my witnesses, and they told me that they would be in court. I started playing spades with the guys now. I was still getting only ten minutes on the phone unless Bernard looked out for me with ten or fifteen minutes of his time. I still didn't like the phone man who had lost the fight. He was still fronting like he was really holding it down.

The only reason he became the phone man in the first place because he was fighting his case for the longest or the second longest person who lived on the A side. As people left to either go home or go upstate, the next longest person usually became part of the phone crew, and it would have nothing to do with if you were strong or weak. It really only had to do with how long you were on the A side. If you were weak, sooner or later someone was going to challenge you.

It was almost time to be locked in. I was hoping that I would be going home the next day since my witness, Mo Junior, the Housing Police officer, was going to be in court. Once he verified that I was with him, I was sure that the court would drop the charges.

Well, things didn't go as I thought they would. When I got into the courtroom, my lawyer and the ADA were laughing with each other. They kept laughing as if I weren't there. Someone yelled my name.

When I looked up, there were Vincent, Junior, Ronnie, Andrew, Jackie, Linda (Vincent's girl), and Mo Junior. I was glad to see them and just knew I was going home.

The bailiffs escorted me to the defendant's table. I looked up and saw that the judge wasn't sitting on the bench at this point. There were two court clerks talking together by the bench. The court reporter was sitting in front of his machine. There were also other families waiting for their loved ones to come from the back.

My lawyer came over to me and asked me how I was doing. I asked him if I was going home. He ignored my question and started telling me that he'd spoken to all my witnesses and all agreed with what I was telling him. He still didn't answer my question, so I asked him again if I was going home. He told me he didn't think so because the ADA was taking the case to the grand jury, which meant that the district attorney was seeking an indictment against me for murder in the second degree. Since the charge was murder in the second degree, the ADA wanted to take it to a higher level, which was the Supreme Courts.

I felt sick. My heart dropped. I didn't know what to think, because I really didn't know what he was talking about. The only thing I knew was that I wasn't going home.

Finally, the judge came out, and the court clerk asked everyone to stand. The clerk announced the judge's name as the judge was sitting down. The clerk then read my docket number, which is the number assigned to the case and the charge. When everyone sat down, the judge read over the charge. He asked the ADA to present his case. A lot of things were going on. A lot of words were spoken. I didn't understand any of it. They might as well have been speaking Chinese. I remember only two things: "no bail" and "remand."

I was so out of it mentally, spiritually, physically, and emotionally that I forgot that Jo Jo was in court with me that day. Jo Jo also had a court-appointed lawyer, whose name was Mr. Fink. After the ADA finished presenting his argument, the judge denied bail and remanded us. We didn't get the opportunity to present our case. The case was going up to the grand jury for an indictment. The ADA had forty-five days to come back with an indictment, or else the case would go back to criminal court, where the case would be dismissed and treated as a misdemeanor.

I was in shock. Tears started coming down my face. I looked around and saw my family watching me. I didn't know what to say. The court clerk came over to our table and told us we had to go. They handcuffed us and escorted us back to the holding pens. They didn't give me a chance to say good-bye to my family. The only thing we did was nod at each other. It was the loneliest day of my life because it felt like I was leaving the world and there wasn't any return.

When my lawyer came to see me, I asked him what it meant that the ADA had forty-five days to get an indictment. He told me that the ADA would present the murder charge to the grand jury for an indictment. I asked him could I present my case to the grand jury, and he told me it wouldn't make any sense because they were going to indict me. I didn't want to hear that, so I got mad. I asked him what he meant by saying it wouldn't make sense to present my case to the grand jury. He told me the ADA had witnesses who placed me at the scene of the crime. I asked him, what about my witnesses? He said that we had to go to court to prove my case. After my lawyer left, I stayed waiting to go back to the facility for about five hours. I was really upset.

Once I got to Atlantic Avenue, the only thing I wanted to do was get on the phone. I didn't want to hear anything from anybody. I asked Bernard if he could look out for me. He told me he would let me know.

I heard a bunch of noise coming from the dayroom. When I looked in, there was a circle, and two individuals were sparring. I went in to see who they were. Two new guys were sparring. You could tell if a person could fight by watching him spar. I could tell neither of these guys could fight, so I left and went back to stand by the phones. I needed to get on the phone so I could call Jackie.

I heard the CO yelling "On the rec," which meant recreation. Rec consisted of being escorted to the eleventh floor, where the gym was located, or the roof where you could get some fresh air. I always went to the gym because basketball was my game. I was pretty nice too. I was hoping that everyone went to rec so that I could get on the phone faster. The same phone man who'd lost the fight got on the phone for about forty-five minutes. I wanted to kick his butt myself. I didn't like him from the beginning, but especially now that he was blocking me from getting on the phone.

I decided to go to my cell and lie down. I was depressed. I had no information about what was going on with this murder charge. Jo Jo wasn't telling me anything. He maintained that he didn't do the murder. I kept asking him what was happening, but all he told me was that the guy who identified him at the scene of the crime was lying. I didn't question him on his whereabouts because I wasn't thinking on that level. I was really frustrated. Not having the answers was killing me.

I must have fallen asleep because the next thing I heard was the CO yelling "On the chow." I couldn't believe I'd slept the whole day without getting on the phone. I must have been really tired from being in court all day without resting or taking a nap.

When I got in the dayroom, a line was already formed, so I just got on the line and waited to get my meal. The meal consisted of cold eggs, toast, corn flakes, and milk. I was really hungry; I don't remember eating at all the day before. One thing about being incarcerated, everything repeats itself. The routine was the same and the food was the same. There was a four-week menu rotation, which started all over again after the fourth week. But I was definitely hungry, so I got my food and sat in the corner.

After chow, they would be calling the morning rec. I wasn't going, because I wanted to get on the phone. I knew Jackie was probably worried about why I hadn't called the night before.

Jo Jo was calling me from the B side gate. Someone came into the dayroom and asked for Herb. I told him my name was Herb. He told me someone wanted me on the B side gate. The B side was right across from the A side. When I got to the A side gate, Jo Jo asked me to come to the gym. I told him I was trying to get on the phone. He understood, but he insisted I go to the gym because he wanted to talk to me about something. So when the CO called rec, I decided to go to the gym to see what Jo Jo had on his mind.

When I got to the gym, Jo Jo wasn't there yet, so I started playing basketball. He finally showed up, so I stopped playing ball. He told me, "When we get to court, don't let the ADA separate the cases." I didn't know what he was talking about. He must have been talking to someone about the case because in prison there are a lot of jailhouse lawyers. Some of these lawyers are legitimate, but some just want to rob you and your family out of their money.

We only got an hour in the gym. When I got back from the gym, I thought about what Jo Jo had said. It just didn't feel right with my spirit because I felt that he was hiding something. After a while, I just forgot about it until he brought it back up again.

I still didn't get on the phone. I asked the phone man when I could, and he told me he would let me know. I stood right there and waited until he called me. The next thing I heard was "On the count."

There were three counts a day. The CO would wake us up for breakfast at about 6:00 a.m. We were back in our cells until about 11:00 a.m. Once they finished the count, they let us back outside our cells until the next count at 4:00 or 5:00 p.m. The last count was at 11:00 p.m. Everyone was in his cell for the night after that last count.

Anyway, I still had not gotten on the phone. Those phone people were playing games, and I was tired of it. Yes, Bernard was looking out for me, but he could not do it all the time. When I finally got on the phone and called Jackie, she wasn't there, so I called the phone booth around the neighborhood to find out what was going on. Someone picked up, but I didn't know him.

I decided to call Mo Junior. He told me that he'd spoken to my lawyer and said to stay strong. I told him that I would remain strong, but I wanted to go home. He told me not to worry about anything. Things would be fine. I wished I could believe him, but I just didn't feel that way. In fact, I felt totally the opposite. I truly felt like I wasn't going home for a very long time.

The phone man started yelling at me that my phone time was over. I stayed on the phone for about another ten minutes while the phone man kept screaming at me. At one point, he left and came back yelling at me in the face. I told him he'd better get out of my face. He just walked away, saying that my time was over. I got off the phone about five minutes later. It was good talking to Mo Junior because he gave me a little hope. It wasn't much, but I felt a little better.

After I got off the phone, I went into the dayroom to watch TV or play spades with the guys. I decided to try to call Jackie again to make sure she was still coming to see me the next day. Jackie had a problem with bringing my daughter to visit me. According to her, she didn't want to expose our daughter to that environment. I didn't understand, because to me it wasn't about the environment, it was about me wanting to see my beloved child. I was there when she was born. And up until that time, I was always in my daughter's life. She used to love going out with me. When I didn't take her, she would cry.

Taneé Murray was born January 26, 1978. I remember that day like it was yesterday because it was the happiest day of my life. She was about thirteen months old when the detectives busted into my house to arrest me. I'd been in the Atlantic Avenue facility for about two months now. Taneé was now about fifteen months, and I didn't want to hear that mess from Jackie. It was crazy! But what could I do or say at that point? I had to go along with her because I had no choice.

On the other hand, I understood where she was coming from because no child should be exposed to an environment like prison. While incarcerated, I soon learned that there was a lot going on in the visiting room. Guys were having sex with their girlfriends. You don't want to expose your little girl to that. Those guys didn't care one way or the other. The only thing they were concerned about was getting their rocks off. I have seen plenty of fights in the visiting room too because guys were being disrespectful to other people's families and kids. At first I didn't understand until I saw what went on in that visiting room firsthand. But I still wanted to see my baby girl. I missed her like crazy. I came to understand that you really don't miss someone until that person is taken away from you. I hoped that Jackie would change her mind.

I reached Jackie on the phone, and she informed me that she was coming but without my daughter. I was glad she was coming, so I didn't argue with her. The phone guy was threatening me to get off the phone. When I finally hung up, I saw the phone guy from the corner of my eye looking as if he wanted to jump me. I wasn't going to allow those phone guys to treat me any way they wanted. I was ready to get busy, especially with the phone guy who'd lost the fight. He was fronting more and more as time went along. I knew he was a coward.

When I got off the phone, I went into the dayroom and started playing spades with the guys. I played cards until it was time to be locked in. The ADA had another fifteen days before I went to court. I just hoped that they wouldn't indict me because I didn't know what I would do next. I just had to pray. The CO called the lock-in, and we proceeded to our cells.

I noticed that we had to lock ourselves in our cells while the CO was in the front of the gallery opening the cells electronically. I thought how crazy it was to be charged for a murder I didn't commit and locking myself into a cell. If you refused to lock the cell door behind you, the CO would write a disciplinary report on you. What?

The time was getting to me. I wanted to go home. I didn't know when my court date was because the ADA was waiting for the indictment to be handed down.

Murder. Every time I thought about it, I got so upset that I wanted to fight. Words can't really explain what I was going through. I was handling it to the best of my ability.

The Indictment

Oh no! I had just received a letter from my lawyer informing me that I was indicted on two counts of murder in the second degree. Unbelievable! Could anything else happen to me, besides dying? Two counts? Why two counts of second-degree murder? They didn't mention anything about two murders! This was getting more confusing. The lawyer also told me that I had to appear before the New York State Supreme Courts the following week to be arraigned on two counts of murder. I was mad!

After reading the letter, I went back downstairs to the dayroom. There was a circle, and that meant that someone was sparring. I stood around the circle. One of the guys sparring was the phone man I didn't like; the other was a new guy who had just come in.

The phone guy got the best of the new guy. I think that was because the new guy was scared and didn't know anyone. He had only been in the facility for about three days, and that was one way some guys got extorted by certain individuals. They played off people's fears. If they saw you a little scared, they would take advantage of you.

One of the guys that I played cards with tried to push me in the middle of the circle. I kept telling him that I don't play with my hands. He kept pushing me toward the center of the circle until I was finally in front of the phone guy I didn't like. The phone guy tried to front by saying that I was scared. I just kept saying to them that I didn't play with my hands. So the guy started punching my body. I didn't have any choice but to defend myself. With my first punch I hit him right in the face as hard as I could. Immediately after that, he quit. He was mad because I wasn't supposed to hit him in the face. He walked off like a little girl.

From that point on, whenever I got on the phone, he would never tell me my time was up. I later apologized to him for hitting him in the face. I told him it was an accident. He said it was all right, but the job was accomplished. At least when he ran the phone, I got more time.

Everyone was calling me by my name. I was slowly but surely getting more time on the phone. After I punched the phone guy, everyone who was in the circle that day saw that I could handle myself. They started giving me respect not only for fighting but also for my basketball skills. I didn't care anything about that stuff, because I wanted to go home. Finally, I was informed that I would appear in court in a couple of weeks to be arraigned on two counts of murder. I still couldn't get over that. I kept asking myself why two counts?

The day I went to court, it was the same procedure as far as getting up really early in the morning so I could eat breakfast, be processed in the receiving room, and be on time for court even though they never called me in the morning. They always called me in the late afternoon every time I went to court. When I got into the court, everyone was in his or her place. When the judge came into the courtroom, everyone stood up, and the court clerk announced the judge presiding over the case. The judge's name was Picus, and he was a no-nonsense judge. He seemed to favor the ADA because every time the ADA submitted a motion, the judge accepted it. But every time my lawyer submitted a motion, the judge would deny it. It was horrible how this judge treated me.

Anyway, my lawyer submitted a motion for bail. The judge set my bail at $150,000. I was shocked! How could I get out when my bail was $150,000? Wasn't bail supposed to be set according to how much income you earn a year? I don't think I was making $25,000 a year, and this judge had the nerve to set my bail at $150,000! Unbelievable!

The judge set Jo Jo's bail at $250,000 because he had prior arrests and felonies. I had a previous felony myself when I was arrested with Jo Jo and the four other individuals. That judge had given us all five years probation. At the end of the five years, my case was sealed. However, Jo Jo had violated his probation, and that was why the judge set Jo Jo's bail at $250,000.

The indictment also charged us with first degree robbery and criminal possession of a weapon in the second degree. The case was postponed until a week later. My lawyer informed me that he would come to the area in the back where the prisoners were being held to explain what just happened in the courtroom. He knew I was confused. I couldn't get over the fact that that the judge had imposed $150,000 bail on me! I didn't really understand until then how much trouble I was in.

When I spoke to my lawyer, he finally explained to me that the reason why the jury indicted me on two counts of murder was because the ADA wasn't sure of the motive. Therefore, the ADA presented the case to the jury with two possible motives. One motive was felony murder. Felony murder was when an individual robbed someone and while he was fleeing from the crime, he commits another felony, in this case, murder. The other motive was common law murder and that's when someone commits murder with no known motive. All this information confused me even more. I asked about bail and he told me that this was a tough judge and that he would request a new bail when we appeared in court the following week.

I realized that there was no way that I was going home anytime soon. My lawyer tried to encourage me by telling me that everything was going to be all right. I didn't want to hear that, because I was being shipped back to jail while he was going home. He also informed me that he would hire a private detective to interview all my witnesses and make an attempt to interview the ADA's witnesses. I asked what he meant by the private detective interviewing the ADA witnesses. He told me that the ADA's witnesses didn't have to respond to the private detective's interview. I also asked him what was going to happen when we got back to court next week. He told me that he was going to submit a motion to the court to have the ADA turn over all his evidence against me.

As far as I was concerned, he wasn't telling me anything I wanted to hear. I was hurting inside. I wondered what was going on. I still didn't have a clue. Jo Jo still wasn't saying much of anything. I started to dislike Jo Jo because something inside me kept saying that he'd had something to do with this crime. I just didn't have anything to support my gut feeling. The next week court date was to determine what kind of evidence the ADA had against me and to try to get my bail reduced from $150,000. I never had that kind of money in my life.

While I waited to be transferred back to Atlantic Avenue, there were several individuals fighting their cases. Sometimes the court proceedings would stress people out to the point where some would ask to go straight upstate to do their time. The majority of prisoners cop out because they lose patience, and often their court-appointed lawyers encourage them to cop out. I don't remember if a copout was offered to me. I don't believe it was because that was only my second appearance before the Supreme Court.

I had been in Atlantic Avenue for almost six months when I found out that my brother was involved with this murder. One day I called the phone on the corner of Adelphi and DeKalb Avenue, and one of the guys told me what was being said on the block regarding the murder. This was someone close to my family, and he said that my brother Anthony, Jo Jo, and Marty were hanging out that day and they wanted money to purchase drugs. Jo Jo allegedly told Marty that he would be back with some money. My brother Anthony was supposed to have left with Jo Jo.

I asked Jo Jo about what I'd heard, and he kept saying that he didn't do anything. He did mention that he was hanging out with my brother that day, but they didn't commit any murder. I asked Jo Jo why he didn't mention that before, and he told me he forgot. What did he mean he forgot? What kind of nonsense was that? I wanted to kick Jo Jo's butt because I knew from that point on that he was holding out on me. Now I had to make a decision about the information I'd received about my brother. I really didn't know how true the information was. I just knew something was wrong. I had to stay on Jo Jo and try to get as much information out of him as I could.

Should I tell my lawyer about the information I'd received? Should I tell on my brother? I loved my brother. I didn't want to see my brother go down for a murder that I wasn't sure that he committed either. I had five witnesses: a housing police officer, a cook, a fire inspector for the New York Housing Projects, my boss (who was also a Lutheran minister), and my two co-workers who all said that I was with them when the murder was committed. I knew that it was just a matter of time before the court realized that they had made a mistake. At least I was hoping it would go that way.

I knew I had to get the truth from Jo Jo, but now my brother was involved. How crazy was that? I was really confused about how to deal with my brother. He never tried to come and see me, write, or even send me a dollar. But it really didn't matter because I knew I hadn't done anything and if he did it; that was on him.

I finally got back from court, and the same stuff was going on. I was fed up with the whole routine of being incarcerated. How can anyone get used to being in jail? It was just like being locked up like an animal. There were many who adjusted to incarceration as just a regular part of life because they were constantly in and out of prison. Some of the guys were there five or six times in their lifetime. I will speak more about that in a later chapter.

The phone man I didn't like was running the phone. I asked him to call me when he got a chance. He told me he would, so I went into the dayroom. They were watching the news. News became a part of our existence as far as keeping track of what went on in the street. We were caged in. The only way we saw any light was when we went to the roof for recreation. It was only an hour. The COs gave us a choice for our rec time: either the gym or the roof. They wouldn't allow both. It was crazy because some would go on the roof just to look down and hope to see a girl walking by. They would yell down at the girl, calling her all types of names: "hey, mama;" "hey, beautiful." And when the girl wouldn't respond, they would cuss and call her names. It was definitely wigged out.

The private detective came to visit me. I told the same story that I had told a thousand times. He told me he would interview all my witnesses and get a signed report from each one of them. I didn't realize that all this investigation was in preparation for the trial. As time went by, I started letting the lawyer take care of everything instead of really knowing what was going on. I just went along.

Prison life was growing on me because I was getting weed from a person who was visiting me. Every time I got weed, I would smoke with Bernard. That was how I started getting a half-hour on the phone. Sometimes Bernard would have me run the phone for him. The more I became involved with everything that was going on in prison, the more I lost track of what was going on with my case.

One day I came from my visit and I told Bernard to meet me at my cell so that we could smoke. When he got there, he brought three other guys. I asked Bernard who were these guys, and he just told me they were with him. I guess he did not understand that you shouldn't bring people with you who were not invited. Bernard was dead wrong for bringing those guys to my cell without asking me. I told him I wasn't lighting up, and he started calling me all types of names. I was kind of intimidated because he was pretty big. Everyone was scared of Bernard, but when I first came into the block, he just looked out for me on the strength. He never gave the impression he was a bully or one of those who go around intimidating individuals. I always thought he was just a good person.

When I told him I wasn't lighting up, he wanted to fight. He told me that I wasn't getting any more phone time besides the ten minutes that everyone else was getting. We started arguing, one thing led to the next, and we started fighting like our lives depended on it. I knew my life depended on it because the phone was my only communication with my family. I wasn't going to let that happen. I came from a fighting family. I had to know how to fight where I came from.

I think my fight with Bernard was the longest fight of my entire life. We got the best of each other. One thing about standing up for yourself, the fight is more than just winning or losing. You will fight even though the odds are against you. People will respect you whether you win or lose. When the COs broke up the fight, they locked Bernard and me in our cells so that we could cool off. The CO didn't want to bother with writing a misbehavior report. Bernard and I were only about six cells away from each other. We started talking, and he apologized. That was my second victory being in there. My confidence was growing every day.

I was involved in running the TV too. I watched whatever program I wanted, and those who were behind me had to watch what I was watching. Most of the new guys usually sat in the back.

After the fight, Bernard and I weren't as cool as before. I believe he was waiting to be sentenced. I heard that he was eventually sentenced to seventy-five years to life. Unbelievable! A lot of us were facing that kind of sentence. I was indicted for two counts of murder. Each count was a minimum of fifteen or twenty-five years to life. I was also indicted for robbery in the first degree and criminal possession of a weapon. First degree robbery was a maximum of twenty-five years. The criminal possession of a weapon carried four years. So I was facing seventy-nine years to life for a crime that I didn't commit.

The Wade and Bail Reduction Hearing

The Wade hearing was to determine who identified me at the scene of the crime and to determine if that identification was admissible in court. When I got to court, I noticed it was the same judge from the last time. I asked my lawyer about that, and he told me that that was the judge appointed to the trial. The judge would preside over all the hearings. I instinctively felt that I was in trouble because this judge favored the ADA.

One person identified me at the scene of the crime. This witness indicated that he'd been on his way down to the subway to cash in a thirty-five-cent token. When he came out of the subway, he saw two individuals running up the stairs. According to this witness, one of these men was tucking what appeared to be a gun down his pants. He identified me as the person who was putting the gun down his pants. The witness said he was coming from a shop where he bought an amp that weighed between thirty and forty pounds.

His testimony was so incredible that I don't know how the ADA believed him from the start. In fact, this witness said he was walking with another person, but no one could find this person anywhere, not even the ADA. The ADA was looking for anybody, it didn't matter if that person was credible or not, to point the finger. Unbelievable!

The ADA's witness said he spoke to Jo Jo while I was standing on the side. He said that Jo Jo was going to get some money and would be back to buy some drugs. We all walked toward the Clinton and Washington train stop direction.

Another witness said that she saw me with Jo Jo when Jo Jo was talking to the other witness. Another witness was on the subway platform when he saw a blur or a side portion of a person's face leaning over a body. He identified one of the other individuals I'd been arrested with five years before as leaning over the body.

The police had my picture from when I was arrested with Jo Jo and others five years prior to this murder. These witnesses picked me out of the picture lineup because they thought I was my brother. Jo Jo mentioned that he was hanging out with my brother that day. Jo Jo even had my brother as an alibi witness. I started putting pressure on Jo Jo. Every time I saw Jo Jo, we would argue to the point that where we were about to fight. I wanted to fight because I knew in my spirit that he was involved one way or another with this murder.

That was all the evidence that the ADA presented to the court, and he gave my lawyer copies of everything. I was mad. My lawyer also presented a motion to have my bail reduced. You wouldn't believe how much the judge reduced my bail to: from $150,000 to $100,000! I frowned when the judge announced the $100,000. He mentioned that I could put up property. I looked at him like he was out of his mind. What property was he talking about? I was living in Flatbush, and this judge was talking about putting up some property. Was he crazy? I knew I wasn't going home because where would I get $100,000?

The case was adjourned for another month so that the private investigator could continue his work. When I got back to the facility, as usual the guys were doing the same stuff. I went right to my cell because I didn't want to be bothered and just wanted to be left alone. Jo Jo was trying to get me to come up to the gym, but I didn't want to be bothered by anyone.

In my cell I started thinking. My hope was deteriorating because nothing good was coming my way. Every time I went to court, something was against me. Everything favored the ADA. Jackie and I started having problems because she was going through her situation out there with money problems and raising a child by herself. It was hard on her. My spirit was low. Although I was in court when everything was presented, I still really didn't understand what was going on. All those legal terms were like Chinese. There was so much stuff going through my mind, it was like I was going crazy. I fell asleep thinking about the worst thing that could happen to me.

I received another letter from the lawyer saying that another hearing would be held. This hearing was to determine if the evidence presented by ADA would be allowed in court. I didn't understand what he was talking about. He also informed me that I would be in court in a week, and he would explain everything to me. I asked Jo Jo what his lawyer was saying to him, and he told me that his lawyer was sending him some papers. He told me that he would let me see them when he got them. Jo Jo and I were still having our battles because I wasn't giving up on the idea that he knew something.

I also found myself getting into trouble, arguing with the CO and fighting whoever got in my way. I just didn't care. If anyone got in my way, I was fighting. I controlled the phone like it was my own. I took hours at a time without anyone saying anything to me. I really didn't have any legal matters I needed to take care of, because I was going to court on a regular basis, so I didn't need to call my lawyer.

I was calling everyone who had a phone. I called the neighborhood pay phone to find out what was going on in the street. I was asking some of the guys who were there to hook me up with their sister or friends of their girlfriends. I used to have this girl come and see me who I met her through one of the guys. She was really a nice girl, but she didn't last long because the waiting became too much for her. The females who came to see their men usually didn't last long because the guys would put too much pressure on them. The guys wanted packages, visits, and money, and when the women couldn't accommodate them, the guys would get really upset with them, sometimes even beating them up in the visiting room. On an average, the ladies lasted no more than a year.

Jackie and I were definitely having problems. She informed me that she'd met some guy, and she liked him. She told me she wasn't coming to see me anymore unless it was to bring me clothes for court. I had now been incarcerated for almost a year, and the trial was about to start. Her timing was definitely off because I needed the support. I became angrier as time passed. I felt sick when she told me that. My feelings were numb. I started not to care for myself. If someone looked at me in the wrong way, there would be a problem. I didn't care anymore. I'm sure she couldn't wait until after the trial to cut out on me. I understand that it was a lot of pressure on her, raising a little girl by herself, but really? I hadn't been convicted yet! I didn't understand the move because it was right before the trial when she told me. I didn't want to hear that because it meant that I couldn't see my baby girl.

I was so mad that I was getting into all kind of fights. I even had a fight with one of the COs because we just didn't like each other. I mean we were really fist fighting, not sparring like we did among ourselves but throwing blows. When I was getting the best of him, he took his prison keys out and stabbed me in the head. I was bleeding so bad that they had to rush me to the infirmary. I don't know what happened to that CO because they transferred me to another unit.

Everybody heard about the fight and they gave me more props. It went straight to my head. I really thought I was the man because I knew about everything that was going on inside the facility. I was so much a part of everything that I wasn't even thinking about the trial.

I was at a point where I didn't really care. My hope was dying by the minute. Jackie wasn't coming to see me anymore. She stopped a few months before I got into the fight with the CO. She didn't accept my calls. I wasn't allowed to talk to my daughter. I mean everything was crashing down on me. I think that was my first development of a "death wish." This meant that I could not care less about myself. It extended to the situation if someone did something to me – even if he killed me. I just didn't care. The beast was coming out of me and I didn't know how to get myself back. I didn't know how to manage the anger. I was totally out of control.

The next time I went to court, the evidence my lawyer tried to get suppressed was allowed anyway. Things were getting worse. The judge gave my lawyer a trial date. The next time I appeared in court, my lawyer and the ADA would begin the jury selection process. A panel of twelve jurors would be selected out of possibly three hundred.

The private detective finished his investigation and received written affidavits from each of my witnesses. The ADA wouldn't allow our private detective to interview his witnesses. The lawyer informed me that it didn't matter because he had their written statements from the ADA. When we appeared in court for the Huntley hearing, after all the prosecution witnesses testified, Jo Jo testified and made a fool out of himself. My lawyer told me that the judge didn't believe anything Jo Jo said because he stumbled through his testimony. I asked Jo Jo what happened, and he told me that it was too cold in the courtroom and it gave him the chills. I was convinced at that point that Jo Jo and my brother were involved in this murder.

A year had passed, and the truth was coming out slowly but surely. I was convinced that some of the witnesses were telling the truth, but they just had me confused with my brother. Unbelievable! The judge asked me if I was going to testify on my behalf, but I was advised not to because at that point in the proceedings, we were going to trial regardless. I was just hoping that the trial would start soon so that I could convince the jury that they had the wrong man.

After a full day of jury selection, a panel of twelve jurors and two alternates were in place. We were all tired when it was over. Court adjourned.

The Trial

As the trial was about to begin, the indictment had been amended in previous hearings. The judge amended the indictment himself, which was clearly a violation of my constitutional rights. Instead of the indictment's finding that the victim was robbed, the judge changed it to attempted robbery. Now the ADA could still try me on the felony murder. Once the judge dismissed the robbery charge, he should have dismissed the felony murder charge too. Instead, it was decided that I would be tried on felony murder, common law murder, attempted robbery, and criminal possession of a weapon.

As I said before, the ADA's witnesses were lying through their teeth, especially the three main ones. Marty said he saw me with Jo Jo, and supposedly Jo Jo told him that he would be right back with some money. I didn't understand that because what did their conversation have to do with me? Apparently, the ADA was trying to establish that my motive was to go and rob and murder an innocent man for money for some drugs. However, it was established before the trial that I had never in my entire life messed with drugs.

Here I was facing twenty-five years to life because of a witness who said I was standing by Jo Jo when those two were conversing. How could the ADA allow such testimony? How could the judge allow such testimony? This guy was a friend of both my brother and Jo Jo. He was also a heavy drug user. In fact, he was on lifetime parole for selling drugs. He would steal, cheat, or lie to save his own behind if necessary.

The next prosecution witness was a guy named Lucky. He claimed that he carried a fifty-pound amp for approximately ten blocks and then stopped to cash in a thirty-five-cent token. Although he had over three hundred dollars in his pocket, he said he was with this guy named Al, but no one could locate Al anywhere.

The next witness was a lady who lived next door to the witness Marty. She had me and my brother confused, but she seemed the most credible on the stand. She couldn't look at me when she was testifying. She just confirmed Marty's testimony saying she saw all three of us allegedly talking on the corner.

There was a witness who said she saw from her window across the street two people running up the subway stairs. She indicated that she'd seen Jo Jo in the neighborhood before, so that's why she recognized him. She said she never saw me in her life.

There was another witness who was on the opposite platform in the station who stated that he saw me leaning over the body going through the victim's pockets. But during the photograph array, he picked out Malik as the person who was leaning over the body.

The ADA finally called his last witness. She also confused me with my brother. She mentioned that she never saw me before, and she said that she didn't see me running up the subway stairs.

So here it was that two of the prosecution's witnesses testified that I wasn't the one they saw. The ADA was relying heavily on Marty's and Lucky's testimony because only they placed me with Jo Jo. I felt sick. The ADA finally rested his case.

All my witnesses testified. My boss, who was also a Lutheran minister, testified that if I wanted to rob anyone, I could certainly have robbed him. I had keys to his place of business. One of my responsibilities was to open the restaurant every morning at 10:00 a.m. My boss was right because there was plenty of petty cash all over the place. Why take a chance on robbing a complete stranger who might not have any money? That didn't make any sense to me.

The ADA tried to make all my witnesses look like criminals—as if they were the ones who had committed the murder! Why would the system or the courts allow such a thing? The ADA tried to make the housing police officer who said I was with him look like he committed a crime. One of my witnesses had gotten arrested for urinating in public. The ADA tried to make him look like he'd raped someone.

I thought the ADA was supposed to protect the public. Wasn't I a part of the public? I was paying my taxes. Why wasn't I given the benefit of the doubt? I felt as soon as I said that I had a police officer as a witness, the ADA should have considered my innocence. But since the ADA wanted to build up his reputation for getting convictions, he didn't care. The ADA knew those individuals were lying.

Marty made a statement, "I would lie, cheat, or steal to get what I want." Wasn't that the same as the ADA's mentality? He didn't care what he must do to persuade the jury; he wanted that conviction. I felt I wasn't getting any justice from the judge either. Every time there was a conference or sidebar, the judge favored the ADA. There was even a sidebar regarding whether or not I was going to testify.

The ADA wanted to ask me questions about the robbery committed years before with Jo Jo. He wanted to influence the jury's mind with a charge that happened five years before, when I was sixteen. It was even illegal to do so because I was given youthful offence treatment, which meant if I completed the guidelines or stipulations set by the probation department, the case would be sealed and couldn't be used against me. But that judge wasn't trying to hear anything my lawyer presented. The judge wanted a conviction as well. So I decided not to testify on my own behalf.

I was being charged with an attempted robbery, and the ADA wanted to establish that I had a history of robbing people. He wasn't going to explain the circumstances of the earlier case; he was going to portray robbery as my MO. I really don't know how my lawyer felt about my testifying because he never gave his opinion about it. I felt he should have because that was an entrapment. The judge knew it was an entrapment because he even asked me if I was going to testify.

Nevertheless, after the judge gave the jury his charge, the jury was left alone to deliberate. They deliberated for three days and asked the judge if some transcripts could be read back to them. I don't remember what transcripts the jury asked for, but after the transcripts were read back, they continued to deliberate for another half day or so. The court clerk brought the judge a note from the jury indicating that they couldn't reach a verdict. I was in shock. I really thought I was going home because it was apparent to me that the ADA's witnesses were outrageously unbelievable. There was nothing concrete presented. Nothing but a bunch of lies! The judge asked the jury if they were sure that they couldn't reach a verdict, and they responded that they were deadlocked. The lawyers had the opportunity to ask each juror what his or her verdict was. With no surprise, all the white jurors' verdicts were guilty, and all the black jurors said not guilty. The murder charge turned into a racial thing. I couldn't believe it!

Although I really didn't understand it at the time, I was being used just so they could nail someone for killing that innocent man. The judge dismissed the jury, and my case was adjourned for an undetermined time. I would have to go through the same procedures all over again. This was getting crazier and more complicated as time went by. I was hoping that the second trial wouldn't take as long as the first. My lawyer submitted a motion for my bail to be reduced, but the judge denied it and my bail remained $100,000.

Once I got back from court, many of the guys rushed at me and asked me what happened. I told them it was a partial verdict. The jury found me not guilty for the charge of common law murder, but they could not reach a verdict on the charges of felony murder, attempted robbery, or criminal possession of a weapon. I now had to go back to trial on the remaining counts that the jury couldn't reach a verdict on. I went straight to my cell and thought about what happened. I couldn't believe that all the blacks said not guilty and all the whites said guilty. I'd been incarcerated for approximately thirteen months, and I felt numb except for my anger. Tears started coming down my face. Words can't describe how much pain I was suffering. I was depressed for about a week after the trial, and I returned to my old self-destructive behavior.

I got back to running things as though it was my house. I wasn't as strict as the other guys who were on me when I first came in. But running the phone became my hustle. I took cigarettes, money, jewelry, sneakers, or anything else that I thought had some prison value. I watched what I wanted to watch on TV. There were about six of us who held it down. Everyone knew we were tight because when someone came up acting like he wouldn't be pushed around, one of two things happened: he either got jumped or burned out. He'd wind up in another unit, and the same thing might happen to him again because it was happening all over. Only the strong survived in here. You either maintained an attitude as if you were crazy and didn't care, or you became a victim. It was a catch-22.

The only thing I was doing as far as the case was concerned was waiting to hear from a new attorney because the lawyer I had couldn't represent me. It was because of what happened between him and one of the prosecution witnesses. When my lawyer cross-examined Marty, he put so much pressure on him that he said that he "would steal, cheat, or rob if it benefited him." Also, during recess, my lawyer was at the water fountain when Marty approached him saying that he had to say what he said because if he didn't, they would have locked him up. When the recess was over, my lawyer told the judge what happened. My lawyer couldn't become my witness at that point in trial. So the whole conversation was disregarded although that piece of evidence was important.

One night I heard a strange noise coming from the cell next door. The noise was like a gagging sound. I knocked on the wall and asked the person if he was okay, but he didn't respond. The gagging sound grew louder and out of control. I started yelling for the CO. All the inmates got involved in calling the CO because we didn't want the CO on the gallery unless it was for something serious. The CO came running, and sure enough, the inmate in the next cell was trying to hang himself. The CO told me I saved this man's life. If I hadn't called the CO when I did, that inmate would have died. Wow! I found out he'd tried to hang himself because his girlfriend was leaving him.

The Second Trial

I finally got a letter from my new attorney. His name was Frederick Feder. His office was located on Hanson Place and Flatbush Avenue. In fact, his office was in the building known for the big clock in downtown Brooklyn. I used to live a few blocks from there.

Mr. Feder came to visit me at the Atlantic Avenue facility. Right away he told me that he believed in my innocence after reading all the testimony from the first trial, but he needed more time to investigate certain pieces of evidence presented there. I asked him what evidence, and he told me he would let me know.

We were ready to start the second trial. When we went before the judge, the first motion concerned the amendment to the indictment. The judge didn't want to touch that one because if he had declared that it was unconstitutional for the first judge to have amended the indictment, he would have to dismiss the felony murder charge. The first jury had already acquitted me for the common law murder charge. I noticed most of the court clerks were talking about the amendment and they were saying that it was a violation of my rights. But the judge went along with the ADA. So it was established that I would be on trial for felony murder as the top count on the indictment along with the criminal possession of a weapon. The attempted robbery wasn't an individual count because it was included in the felony murder charge.

It was all very confusing. I didn't understand any of it. It was just a bunch of noise to me.

Looking back, not only did the second judge violate my rights as far as the amendment of the indictment, but also he violated my right as far as "double jeopardy," which means that I went to trial two times for the same offense. This was just one of the issues the new lawyer fought against, but we lost the first round.

The second argument that Mr. Feder brought before the judge was regarding the prior robbery in my youth. The judge agreed with my lawyer that that case was sealed, and the ADA couldn't question me about that particular crime. I was happy about that because I could finally tell my side of the story.

The case was adjourned to the following week, when we would begin jury selection. The bailiff escorted me back to the inmate holding area. Mr. Feder came back to see me, and we talked about the case. I told my side of the story, and I guess he was feeling me out so he could see what kind of person I was. He informed me that he would be talking to each of my witnesses. He wanted to become more familiar with them. The CO called, "On the go-back," which meant the bus was there to transport us back to Atlantic Avenue. Mr. Feder told me that he would come to see me at the facility before our next court date.

When I got to Atlantic Avenue, the same stuff was going on. I heard that there'd been a stabbing between one of the phone guys and another inmate. The two fought over the phone, and the phone guy got shanked. A shank might be made out of any object that could be sharpened. When I heard about the stabbing, I was kind of worried because I didn't want to get stabbed. I didn't stop running the phone, but I wasn't as hard as the other phone guys. I always gave extra time on the phone, especially to those who just got busted, because I knew how hard it was when someone first got arrested. Some people were on the phone to inform their families about being arrested. Some were on the phone to try and get bail. There were all kinds of reasons why the phone was important for people who were incarcerated. It was our only line of communication to the outside world.

There were four sides on each floor that housed inmates. Each side had approximately sixty inmates. There was one TV and one phone on each side to accommodate all those people. The whole setup was designed to cause confusion, because how were one TV and one phone going to satisfy that many men without causing problems?

The prison system created a dog-eat-dog environment. Only the strong survived, and the weak perished. I was determined to survive by any means necessary. Although there weren't a lot of stabbings at Atlantic Avenue, they did happen from time to time. Therefore, I became more cautious.

Time went by slowly in prison because things were so repetitive in there. They rotated the same menu week after week. Every Friday we had fish. Every Sunday we had chicken and so on and so on. All the food used to be delivered to each unit, and we ate in the dayroom or in our cells. All the silverware must be returned and counted before the COs allowed us to resume watching TV or using the phones. If any silverware went missing, the CO would lock everyone in his cell so that each cell could be searched. Usually everyone cooperated as far as the silverware was concerned because everyone wanted to go back to the TV or the phone.

Finally, I was scheduled to appear in court for jury selection. When I got to court, the lawyers were all talking to each other while waiting for the judge. I was escorted to the defendant's table. Jo Jo was right behind me. He didn't testify at the first trial, and he wasn't going to testify at the second trial either. His case was moot. He really didn't have a case, and I felt he was holding on to me. I believe he felt that if I got acquitted, he would also be found not guilty.

It made me sick. How could someone just sit there and act like so innocent? The only reason he didn't want to call my brother as a witness was because he didn't want to incriminate himself. I had to worry only about myself. Why worry about someone else when my butt was on the line? I was scared to death because the first trial showed me that it was possible that I could be convicted for this murder. I didn't know what I would do with myself.

The jury and two alternate jurors were selected. The first person to testify for the prosecution was that cat Lucky. He's the one who said he saw me and Jo Jo running up the subway stairs; he'd said he bought an amp weighing fifty pounds and walked so many blocks just to stop at a subway station to cash in a thirty-five-cent token.

When my lawyer questioned him regarding the amp, Lucky stated that he bought the amp from the pawnshop on Flatbush and Atlantic Avenue. He didn't know my lawyer's office was right across the street from that shop. There was a sidebar because my lawyer wanted to investigate the ADA's witness statement. It was decided at the sidebar that my lawyer would be permitted to call the owner of the pawnshop when it was time for me to present my case.

Why didn't my first lawyer investigate this witness statement? Why didn't the private investigator question this witness? My first lawyer certainly had all the ADA witness statements because he gave me copies of each one. So no one took the initiative to talk to the owner of the pawnshop? I was angry. The people from the first trial had railroaded me. I noticed that the judge from the first trial was sitting in the courtroom with the other people. Why was he here? Did he still wish for my conviction?

After Lucky testified, the ADA called Marty to the stand, and he repeated the nonsense testimony he had given at the first trial. Basically every prosecution witness said the same thing that they said at the first trial, except for the one who said he saw me across the platform leaning over the body. He identified one of the individuals who'd been arrested with us five years earlier in a photo array. That witness couldn't testify because he was dead by the second trial.

My lawyer wanted to present the transcripts from the first trial, but the judge wouldn't permit it. Why didn't he allow those transcripts to be read to the second jury? It certainly would have helped me because this witness said he never saw me in his life. The only time he saw me was at the first trial. There really wasn't anything concrete or substantial to tie me to this murder. It seemed clear to me that they just wanted someone to go down for this murder.

After the ADA rested his case, my lawyer presented my case. My witnesses all said the same thing that they said at the first trial. But in this trial, my lawyer called three new witnesses. First, the pawnshop owner testified that the Wednesday that Lucky said he bought the amp from his shop was a lie because the pawnshop was closed on Wednesdays. I could hardly believe what I was hearing. This should have come up in the first trial. I strongly believe that I would have been acquitted if the jury had heard this testimony during the first trial.

Next my lawyer questioned the incident between my first lawyer and Marty when they met during a recess. My lawyer was at the water fountain when Marty came up to him stating that the arresting officers told him if he didn't cooperate with them, he would be locked up for the murder. The ADA tried to make my first lawyer look like he was on trial for the murder. I felt the ADA's case was falling apart because my second lawyer was putting so much pressure on his witnesses that they were stumbling on their testimony.

When it was my time to testify, I was scared to death. The ADA tried to trick me when I was testifying. After I told my story, he questioned my whereabouts on the day of the murder. When I named the people I was with on that day, he asked me something totally contrary to what was said. I was telling the truth, so it didn't matter how many times he tried to trick me. I could have told my story a million times, and I would not have contradicted myself.

After I testified, my lawyer and Jo Jo's lawyer told me I did very well on the stand. Jo Jo's lawyer convinced him not to testify because of the last time. Then we rested our case, and the case was turned over to the jury to deliberate.

The jury deliberated for about three days before they made a request to the court to have some transcripts read back to them. I don't remember which testimonies they wanted read back to them, but it took another day before they came back with a guilty verdict.

How could they find me guilty without any substantial evidence? Words can't describe my state of shock. I felt that it didn't matter who my witnesses were; they wanted a conviction to pay for the death of that innocent man. When that jury came back with a guilty verdict, I only remember crying. Tears started coming down my face uncontrollably. How could they have found me guilty? Both lawyers asked each juror his or her verdict, and everyone said guilty. The jury was dismissed, and my case was adjourned.

I don't remember the sentence date, but it wasn't too far from the time I was convicted, maybe two weeks. I will never forget the day that I was sentenced. When the judge asked me if I had anything to say, tears were coming down my face so much, I couldn't speak. When the judge asked Jo Jo, he went off. He started calling the judge all kind of racial names, saying that the judge railroaded us. I just stood there crying like a baby. I couldn't move. The judge sentenced us to fifteen years to life for the murder and one and a half to four and a half years for criminal possession of a weapon in the second degree. The case was finally closed.

We were transferred back to Atlantic Avenue to wait for a transfer to Rikers Island. From Rikers, we would be shipped to some facility in upstate New York to do our time. Rikers was not like the Brooklyn House of Detention; it was much larger. It must have had four times as many prisoners. Rikers Island was considered the biggest holding facility in the world.

When I got to Rikers Island, I went through the same process I went through when I first got to the Brooklyn House of Detention. I went to the Receiving Room where I was strip-searched and processed into the system. Then I was sent to the House of Detention for Men (HDM), where the population was triple the number in the Brooklyn House of Detention. They sent me to the third tier, which was on the third floor, also known as "Three Block." Everybody there either was going to trial for murder or had been convicted for murder and was waiting to be transferred upstate.

There were many more fights and stabbings on Rikers Island. I don't remember what cell I was assigned to, but it was right next to an individual who was running everything: giving out phone time, distributing tobacco, and running the guys who cleaned up at the end of the night. He was definitely considered the man because everyone respected him to the utmost. He had already been sentenced to twenty-five years to life for murder. Everyone respected him not because he was a nice guy but because he wouldn't hesitate to stab you for anything.

A new guy came in after me, and the CO. placed him in the cell across from the guy who was running everything. The new guy didn't like to take showers, and he smelled. It was a very offensive odor, so the guy who ran everything kept telling this guy to get in the shower. The new guy told him to mind his business. So the guy who ran everything threw water into the new guy's cell, but the guy didn't pay him any mind. Someone ended up setting the new guy's cell on fire. He claimed that the guy who ran everything did it.

When the guy who ran everything was in the dayroom getting his food, the new guy came behind the guy with an iron mop wringer and hit him in the head. I was standing right there when it happened. The guy who ran everything fell flat on his face, bleeding like crazy. I thought he was dead, and out of sympathy I grabbed the new guy when he tried to hit him again.

Friends of the guy who ran everything tried to stab the new guy, but the COs finally came in to see what was going on. They took the guy who ran everything to the hospital. When he came back to the block, they told him what happened. When he found out that his boys didn't react quickly enough, he stabbed four of his so-called friends. They went to the hospital, and the guy who ran everything went to special housing unit (SHU)—isolation.

Everyone in the block heard about the incident, and they gave me respect. I became the man on the block. I wasn't there more than two weeks when this incident happened. There must have been over two hundred people in that block.

The Hispanics had their section in the back of the block, and the blacks had their section in the front of the block. The phones were in the front of the block. The Hispanic people ran their phone, and I ran the phone for the black population. There was a neutral phone in between the black and the Hispanic phone.

I didn't stay on Rikers Island that long because I was just there to be transferred upstate. I heard a lot of stories about the upstate facilities during my stay at Rikers. The stories were very intimidating, especially those like the "booty bandits." These were individuals who would first befriend young guys and then rape them. There were also stories about all the stabbings upstate. They said guys got stabbed for the least thing. I was definitely afraid and didn't want to go upstate. But at the same time, I was determined to survive when I got there. I became determined that if I were confronted with a situation, I would have to put in the work by any means necessary. I wasn't going to let anything happen to me while I was doing my fifteen years to life.

I was at Rikers Island for only a few months before they transferred me upstate. I believe it was September of 1981. The CO told me to pack all my property and said someone would come to take me down to the receiving room to be processed for the trip upstate.

"Prison not only robs you of your freedom,
it attempts to take away your identity."

—Nelson Mandela

Sing Sing

The ride from Rikers Island to Sing Sing was the longest I ever took in my life. It felt like we were never going to get there. While we were on the bus, some of the veterans, the ones who were used to the ride, were talking on the bus. They explained to us young guys why we were going to Sing Sing as opposed to Downstate Correctional Facility. Downstate was closed because it was overpopulated.

When we finally got there, the building looked like an old castle. In fact, I believe Sing Sing is the oldest correctional facility in the state of New York. When we got inside, the CO took us to the reception center. There was nothing welcoming about this reception center. We called it the "dehumanizing center" because they made you feel less than human. There were thirty COs standing in front of thirty boxes. They told everyone to get buck-naked and put our things in a box. We had to stand there, unable to hide any of our private parts, while a nurse came to check everyone and find out if we had to take any medication.

Then two COs with plastic suits and zip guns sprayed us with insecticide (bug spray). One of them told us to turn around and crack them. He wasn't talking about turning around and crack a smile either. He wanted us to turned around and bend over while he sprayed us with this wet insecticide. Then they gave us a bar of soap and a big pair of underwear and took us to the shower. It didn't matter if the water was hot or cold, we were getting in that shower.

Then the CO took us to the barbershop, and all of our hair was cut. We all had bald heads. They also cut off all of our facial hair except for eyelashes and eyebrows. We all looked like Martians who had just landed.

After that, they took us to the receiving room where they gave us a state number. They told us never to forget that number. We needed that number for everything: to use the telephone, to have a visit from family, for the commissary, to go to recreation. That number became my name. Before they called us by our birth name, they would call us by that number, and anyone who didn't answer to that number would have a misbehavior report written up on them.

Once someone got a misbehavior report, they would be sent before the adjustment committee. We called it the "kangaroo court." The committee wanted to adjust your behavior by any means necessary. Depending on the offense, there was a three-tier system. For example, stabbing another inmate was a tier three offence. You could get anywhere from one day to infinity in the Special Housing Unit (SHU).

After we were given a number, the CO took us to the state shop for the state greens. The CO who ran the state shop didn't care about anyone's size. Someone's waist might be 32, but the CO would give them a size 42, and their pants would be falling off their butt. Or you might be a 42, and the CO would hand you a size 38, and your pants would be too tight, and all the booty bandits would be looking at you.

After we left the state shop, the CO took us to our cells. The blocks were way larger than what I ever saw on TV. They had at least four times the number of inmates of the Brooklyn House of Detention and Rikers Island put together. It was a very scary sight, and inmates were yelling all over the place. It was nothing like my experience at Brooklyn House of Detention or Rikers Island. I was in "the Big House," as so many of the old-timers would say. There was so much noise on the block that you couldn't hear anything. Even the CO had to yell when he was giving us an instruction or an order.

When I got into the cell, there was a cot, a sink, a toilet, and a desk. The cell wasn't big enough for a dog to live in. I could straighten my arms out and touch the walls on either side. It was very difficult even do a push-up in the cell because it was so small. I'd been in the cell for about an hour when the door opened. I looked out and noticed that all the inmates were standing outside their cells. The CO was calling the chow, aka dinner.

I think Sing Sing, at the time, had the second largest population out all of the New York state correctional facilities. There were approximately three thousand inmates there, so about fifteen hundred inmates were getting ready to eat at the same time. It was a madhouse when we got to the mess hall.

I don't remember what they were serving my first day there, but the food didn't look bad at all. I do remember a long line to get into the mess hall. Once we got inside, the CO that escorted us would stand by the line and make sure that we just took the ration that we were given out. If a CO wasn't there watching the food, the inmates would steal extra food from the line. If an inmate got caught stealing food, a misbehavior report would be issued for stealing.

After we ate, we went back to the cells, and we were locked in for about an hour until the cells were opened again. It was time for recreation. Recreation consisted of watching TV, playing cards, playing chess, or smoking weed with one of your homeboys. It was too loud to hear the TV, so I went and watched two inmates play chess. We only had two hours for recreation, then it was back to our cells for the night.

The next day we had the opportunity to take recreation outdoors. Each block would alternate between having recreation in the gallery and then the next day having it outside. I was only there for about two weeks before they transferred me to another facility. The CO came to my cell and told me to pack everything up because I was being transferred. I asked him what jail was I going to, and he told me that he couldn't tell. He told me he would be back to pick me up. When he came and got me, he took me down to the receiving room to wait for the bus. No one knew where we were going except for the COs on the bus. It was scary not knowing where we were going. It was like being blindfolded. By the way, Jo Jo was right along with me during this process at Sing

Sing. When we were being transferred, he acted as if it didn't matter with him one way or another.

It took us about nine hours to reach Elmira Correctional Facility. When we got there, Elmira also looked like a castle. The CO took us to the receiving room where we were processed. They didn't take us through the same procedure as Sing Sing because we already had our state identification number. The CO took us straight to the cell block. The cell block was considered reception, where we would be classified. Classification determined what level of security prison we would be sent to.

We were locked in our cells for approximately sixteen hours a day. Our food was served to us in our cells. They didn't want us to mingle with the general population because they didn't know what level of security we were going to be. They didn't want a medium-security inmate mingling with a maximum-security inmate.

They determined our education level. They checked our health to determine if we needed medication or medical assistance. We also met individually with a correctional counselor so that he or she could inform you what was expected of you while being incarcerated. We all had on the same clothes: green pants and green shirts. They made us walk in a straight line. If you deviated slightly, they would scream in your face. If you were black, they called you the most offensive racial slur you can imagine and dared you to challenge them.

All the COs knew each other one way or another. Brothers, cousins, uncles, fathers, mothers, and good friends were all working at the facility from this little town called Elmira. They were white (there wasn't a black correction officer there), and they didn't mind letting you know they would kill you if you get out of control or disrespected any of them.

Until that time, I really had not encountered much racism. In Elmira, all employees were white: the counselors, the teachers, the doctors, the nurses, the volunteers, the reverends. The COs were very intimidating. All of them were big. They were hillbillies. They were former farmers who never came into contact with blacks. They had no idea how to relate to other groups outside their race. When the COs heard us speaking in slang, they would get offended. They took it personally to the point where they would harass us. I will talk about this in a later chapter.

In reception the whole group did everything together. We went to meals together; we went to recreation together; we watched TV together; and when it was time to lock us in our cells, everyone went to his cell. All our activities took place separate from the general population.

The only time the reception inmates came into contact with the general population was on Sundays at religious services. Every religion that was on the outside of prison, they had inside: Catholics, Protestants, Muslims, and the rest. There were more than one sect of Muslims: Sunnis, Shiites, Black American Muslims, and the Nation of Islam. The Five-Percent Nation considered themselves a religion, but at that time the administration didn't recognize them. Years later they were recognized by the courts.

But otherwise, most of the time we spent our time in our cells. Being in a cell sixteen hours a day was torture. The COs allowed us to shower once a day, but when it was hot, like eighty degrees, it was unbearable. Some inmates just couldn't endure the pressure, so they hanged themselves.

After being classified by our correctional counselor, we were individually transferred to a facility. Some of the inmates stayed at Elmira, like my codefendant Jo Jo. Since I told my counselor that I wanted to get my GED, I was classified to a maximum correction facility that promoted education. That facility was Auburn, the second oldest the facility in the state of New York. I was kind of glad that my codefendant and I were being separated.

The Auburn Correctional Facility

Auburn Correction Facility wasn't far from Elmira. It was about an hour's ride to get there. When we approached Auburn, it again looked like a castle. The general population was approximately twenty-eight hundred.

The majority who were there had done violent crimes: they were murderers, rapists, serial killers, police killers ... I mean, all kinds of violent criminals were there, inmates who had seventy-five years to life, 150 years to life, even 200 years to life. You had some people in Auburn who had already been in there 30 years and this was 1981. You do the math. The whole atmosphere of the prison was that only the strong would survive. It was really scary because the majority of the inmates didn't care if they lived or died. Many of them didn't harm themselves but thought nothing of killing another person. You had the choice of living or dying.

I came upstate with fifteen years to life for a crime that I didn't commit. I was determined to survive. Mind you, I was only twenty-three years old with the mentality of a fourteen- or fifteen-year-old.

Once the CO gave the transfer papers to the administration office, he escorted us to the identification office where our pictures were taken and an identification card was given to each of us. The CO told us that if we ever lost our identification card, we had to pay for the card and we would receive a misbehavior report. The identification card had the prisoner's picture, state number, and birth name.

After we left the administration building, the CO escorted us to the cell block that housed the reception inmates, and we had to go through the yard to get to the cell blocks. There were hundreds of inmates in the yard. Those who were hanging out close to the administration building just stopped and looked at us. They wanted to see if they knew anyone who was just coming into the facility. The CO continued to usher us on because new inmates had to see the sergeant before they were allowed into the general population. Once the new inmates came into the facility, the sergeant had seventy-two hours to speak with them.

The facility was divided into five cell blocks. A Block housed inmates who were working in the plate shop and cab shop. The majority of New York State license plates were made in the plate shop at Auburn. Desks and chairs were also made in the cab shop. The inmates who worked at these shops were paid the most out of all the jobs in the facility. If my memory serves me right, I think it was 32 cent an hour.

B Block housed inmates who were working in the mess hall. These guys were the riffraff of the jail, and the mess hall became their hustle. They would steal anything that wasn't nailed down and sell it to the general population. Cigarettes became their main commodity as far as prison money was concerned. Everything illegal was done with cigarettes.

C Block housed inmates who were assigned to the school building. These inmates were trying to obtain their GED or pursue a vocational trade like electrical, plumbing, or auto mechanic or one of the other programs offered in the school building. These inmates were trying to get themselves together with an education.

E Block housed the inmates who had the good jobs in the facility, but they didn't get paid much. They worked in the administration building or the visiting room or were teacher's aides. E Block was the honor block. E Block was the cleaner block. Everyone wanted to live in E Block. Those inmates were allowed to have extra recreation time during the weekends because they were the honor inmates.

D Block was the dirtiest and the noisiest block. This block housed the majority of inmates in reception. They were either coming into or leaving the facility. It was crazy in there when the CO took us in. Inmates were on their cell bars screaming and trying to be heard over the other screaming inmates. It was a madhouse. I couldn't believe it, and I was scared to death. Hundreds of inmates must have been in their cells that night when I came through.

I was escorted to the third company, cell 46. My first location at Auburn Correctional Facility, a maximum security prison, was D-3-46. When the CO closed the cell door, it sounded like I was never ever going to get out. It felt like my life was gone. There was nothing more I could do to make it stop. Why was this happening to me?

The sergeant finally came to see me two days later. He asked me two questions: Did I want to go to protective custody? And did I have any enemies in the facility? How in the world did I know if I had any enemies in this jail? I had never been to Auburn in my life. In fact, I had never been incarcerated before. It was all a trap. Those hillbillies didn't care anything about my life.

Once the sergeant left my cell, I was allowed to go to the general population. The sergeant instructed me never discuss my personal business with anyone. I just sat in my cell for about an hour because I didn't know what to do. I was definitely intimidated. I didn't see anyone I knew when I was being escorted to the cell block. The only thing I saw was a bunch of inmates watching TV by the administration building.

I heard the CO yelling and asking me if I was going to the yard or staying in my cell. I guess I was forced to go to the yard because I didn't want to remain in that small cell. All my personal property was taken from me when I came into the facility. Therefore, I had nothing—no personal care items, no food, no change of underwear, nothing. I was walking very slowly because I was scared. I didn't know where the yard was, and I didn't want to ask the CO because he was looking at me like I was the scum of the earth. Clearly he didn't like me at all. The COs in Auburn were more racist than the ones in Sing Sing or Elmira, although Elmira came close. At least in Sing Sing there were a lot of black officers.

When I got to the yard, I still didn't see anyone I knew. I just stood on the side and watched TV with the rest of the guys. Everyone knew I was a new Jack because of my bald head. While I was watching TV, I noticed the CO on the roof walking back and forth with his M16 rifle. There were hundreds of inmates in the yard. I just stood on the side hoping no one would mess with me. My mind was set that if someone messed with me, I was going to defend myself by any means necessary.

I saw one of the guys who came with me from Elmira and we started talking. He asked me if I wanted to walk around the yard. I didn't want to move from where I was because I was safe. No one messed with me there, and I wanted it to remain that way. So I told my newfound friend that I was all right where I was. He kept asking me to walk around, especially to the other yard. I decided to do so.

The yard that I was in consisted of basketball courts, five TVs, a shower house, and a baseball field. There was a long line of inmates standing by the door of the commissary. Someone told me that every time you go to commissary, you had to come into the yard. And some of the inmates would watch you to see how much money you spent by the weight of the bag or number of bags you were carrying. The first thing that came to my mind when I heard this was that I might have to fight someone because I wasn't going to let anyone take anything from me.

So my new friend and I went to the other yard. It was much bigger than the other yard. It had weight courts, handball courts, a shower house, and the "hangout" courts. Every group had a hangout court: the Muslims, the Spanish, the whites, groups of guys from Brooklyn and other boroughs, guys from upstate New York, Christians, and so forth. No one could violate another group court because it would start a riot in the yard.

If an inmate wanted to go on another group's court, he had to get permission. The same procedure applied to the weight courts. No one could violate another group's weight court because it could start a riot. The reason why the courts were so protected was because the inmates would hide knives (shanks) on other group's courts. If the CO searched any court and found a weapon, he would destroy the court. Therefore, for the most part, inmates respected the courts.

Let me explain something about going from one yard to the next. Inmates had to go through a tunnel where there was a blind spot where the CO couldn't see; therefore, a lot of inmates would get stabbed going through the tunnel. You definitely had to be careful.

I heard the CO calling chow through the PA system. If inmates wanted to go to dinner, they had to go through the yard. Those inmates who didn't come outside for recreation were allowed to come to the yard to go to the mess hall to eat. I don't remember what we ate that day, but I do remember saying that the food wasn't that bad compared to the food at the Brooklyn House of Detention or Rikers Island.

When the mess hall closed, the CO called the yard closed, and all the inmates had to return to their cells for the evening count. There were four mandatory facility counts, at 6:00 a.m., 11:00 a.m., 5:30 p.m., and 11:00 p.m. If an inmate was not in his cell for a count, he would immediately be sent to the Special Housing Unit (the SHU) and issued a misbehavior report. He could receive one day to infinity in the box.

Once the CO took the count, those inmates who had night programs had to get ready for their programs. Inmates who didn't have any night programs had to remain in their cells. D Block didn't have any recreation that night. Therefore, we remained in our cells for the remainder of the night. Since dinner was over at about 5:30 p.m., we would be in our cell until about 6:30 a.m., when the CO would open the cell doors for breakfast. Those were some long nights being in that cell. Some inmates couldn't stand the pressure of being in their cell that long and would hang up. They would kill themselves. Sometimes those walls felt like they were closing in on me, but I learned in later years that reading was my escape from those walls.

I didn't have any of my personal property in the cell because it had been confiscated by the facility property officer for search when I entered the facility. I had absolutely nothing in my cell. I was looking at the walls trying to go to sleep, but I couldn't. I think that was the saddest day in my life because I felt lost. I felt locked in. I felt the world was coming down on me. My level of hope was almost at zero, and I didn't know what to do. I just lay on that hard bed thinking all kinds of stuff.

Right before I came upstate, I rehired Mr. Feder as my appeals lawyer. I thought that since he was already familiar with my case, why not. I believe he charged me four thousand dollars to take on the case. I remember lying there thinking that I still had a chance of getting out. I'd been railroaded. I didn't belong in prison. I had witnesses, and what better witness than a police officer to verify my whereabouts? I thought about the family of the victim. Did they really believe I was the one who killed their loved one? They were at the trial. They heard all the witnesses. Did they really believe the prosecutor's witnesses over a police officer, or did they just want someone to pay whether or not that person had committed the crime? I know that the first trial's judge wanted a conviction and didn't care how it came about. If all my jurors had been white at the first trial, I would have been convicted. They wanted someone to pay, and I was that person. What a shame!

I finally fell asleep, and the next thing I knew, the CO was calling chow (breakfast), and those who had morning program had to leave their cells. Those who didn't have morning program were allowed to come back to their cell. Rec wasn't mandatory; therefore, an inmate could remain in his cell if he wanted. Every inmate must have two programs while incarcerated. The programs were broken down in three tiers: morning program, afternoon program, and evening program. If an inmate refused a program, a misbehavior report would be issued. I was told that I had to see the program committee the following morning.

The program committee was set up to assign every inmate with a program that would help him with his adjustment such as a vocation program or academic program. I didn't have my GED or a vocational trade. My academic program would be from 8:00 a.m. to 11:00 a.m., and the vocational program was from 12:30 p.m. to 3:30 p.m.

When I got back from the program committee, the block CO informed me that my correctional counselor wanted to see me at 1:30 p.m. A correctional counselor was assigned to every inmate upon coming into the facility. The correctional counselor's primary responsibility was for the inmate to know what was expected of him while being incarcerated. The counselor evaluated the inmate every three months. If the inmate conformed to the rules and regulations of the facility, he could request to be transferred to a facility that was closer to his family. However, if the inmate got into trouble, he would remain right there, maybe nine or ten hours from his loved ones.

My correctional counselor didn't appear to be a bad person. After I explained my circumstances to him, he was shocked by my story. In fact, he couldn't believe what had happened to me, even with my case file right in front of him. He kept asking me about the police officer who indicated that I was with him on the day of the crime. He just shook his head and continued going through the procedures with me.

He was telling me about the first stage of incarceration. He said most inmates who came upstate were in the denial stage: The denial stage begins when the person enters prison. It generally lasts between one and three years for long-timers (those sentenced to more than ten years). Some short-timers remained in a state of denial for their entire sentence. Prisoners in the denial stage find it hard to believe that they are really in prison. They focus their energy on filing appeals, schemes to escape, and dreams about the outside world. They feel that they are somehow different from all the other prisoners. Some prisoners work through the denial stage gradually. Over time, they become more and more aware of reality. Others in the denial stage abruptly change when they face a crisis such as a rejected appeal or a problem with a loved one.

After the correctional counselor finished telling me about how inmates adjust in prison, he told me that he would call me back in a month. He also told me that if I kept my nose clean, I should be all right. He didn't know I had already made up my mind that I would be all right by any means necessary.

When I left his office, I went to the yard where I met some of the guys who came on the bus with me. They also went to the program committee and received their programs. One of the guys who had his high school diploma got a job working in the plate shop. Making license plates was the best job in the facility because they paid the most. I had tried to get a job in the plate shop, but they wouldn't give it to me because I needed my GED.

There wasn't really anything to do in the yard but walk around and see the sky. I couldn't see anything beyond the thirty-foot wall that surrounded the entire jail. I couldn't see any cars, people, or anything. While most of the inmates were at a program, there weren't many people in the yard. Those who were there were working out on the pull-up bar or lifting weights. When I walked past the weights, I noticed that some of the guys were really big dudes. I mean they were huge.

It was around 11:00 a.m., and the CO was closing the yard. Again everyone must return to his cell. All programs were closed.

After the CO made his eleven o'clock count and the administration cleared it, we were allowed to go to chow (lunch). When I got to the mess hall, there were two lines for inmates to receive their food. One line consisted of inmates who were either Hispanic or whites and a handful of blacks. The other line consisted mostly of blacks. When I was in Brooklyn House of Detention and Rikers Island, the population wasn't as segregated as it was upstate. Auburn Correctional Facility was totally segregated in the year 1981. The Attica riot was just ten years before my coming to Auburn and some of the inmates who were in the riot were at Auburn when I got there.

I sat down at a steel table facing another inmate while eating. The inmates had a rule among themselves that if an inmate wanted to turn his back on the person opposite him, he must knock on the table to excuse himself. Well, this particular inmate who I was sitting next to didn't excuse himself, and the inmate that was sitting across from him stabbed him in the neck with a fork. I wasn't in Auburn more than two weeks before I saw my first real stabbing. I had never seen anything like it in my life! The inmate who got stabbed just ran to the closest

CO for assistance, but the CO was frightened for his own life and ran. I could hardly believe what I'd just witnessed, but it certainly taught me a valuable lesson: I needed to knock before I turned my back on an inmate in the mess hall.

The COs locked everyone in the mess hall until the investigation was over and then escorted all the inmates back to their respective blocks. I was still shook behind what happened when I got back to my cell. All programs and recreation were cancelled until further notice. I had just received my personal property a little earlier, so at least I had a few books I could read until they let us out of our cells.

I was sitting on my bed when a sergeant and a CO came to my cell and asked me what I'd heard and seen in the mess hall. I told them that I didn't see a thing. They said that I was lying because I was sitting right next to the guy who was stabbed, but I stuck to my guns because guys in prison had to mind their own business. This was the first rule among inmates. The sergeant and the CO tried to intimidate me by screaming at me and telling me that I was lying. They finally left my cell, upset that I wouldn't cooperate with them. I wondered why they needed me to cooperate when they knew who did the stabbing. But after that happened, we all stayed in our cells for the night.

There was so much noise in D Block that I couldn't even think. Inmates were yelling from one cell to the next. One inmate who was in cell 14 would be trying to talk to another inmate in cell 35. I kept hearing, "You hear me?" They couldn't hear each other, but they kept trying to talk for hours.

I finally got up the courage to knock on the wall of the inmate next cell from me. I asked him if he had any books or magazines I could read. He gave me a Donald Goines book. It an easy book to read, but honestly, up until that point I had never read an entire book in my life. I couldn't read. I was saying words as opposed to comprehending them. But this book was a gangster book and was very readable. I think I read through the entire collection of Donald Goines books. They kept my mind off the cell walls and bars for a little while at least. Sometimes I did push-ups just to keep my mind occupied. Sixteen hours was a very long time to be in a small cell that wasn't equipped for a dog, let alone a grown man.

When the CO finally let us out of our cells, the whole jail was talking about what had happened except the old timers. One guy was preaching in front of the TV. He said it was a shame that a brother would stab another brother. It was Black-on-Black crime in the prison system. The old-timer was saying that the COs loved it when we killed each other.

Later the guy who I met the day before decided to walk around the yard with me. We were talking about the incident, and I asked him how he felt about the situation. He told me that he thought the incident was crazy, and it scared him. I know it shook me.

Since there was nothing to do in the yard, we walked around in circles from one part of the yard to another or leaned against the wall. Other inmates were lifting weights; some were at the pull-up bar doing pull-ups, push-ups, and dips. Other inmates were playing basketball. This was the life I had to live for the next fifteen years or the rest of my life? Unbelievable!

The CO on the PA system called the yard closed. I was glad because I was tired of being there. Once an inmate was in the yard, he must remain in the yard until it closed. It didn't matter if it was 10 degrees below zero or 102 degrees in the shade.

That night a piece of mail was dropped in my cell. It was from my little brother Joe, who said that he was coming to see me on Sunday. That was definitely good news because I really needed a few things. There was another piece of paper from the mailroom attached to my letter, indicating that I must send my brother a correspondence form for Administration to grant permission for him to visit me. If my brother wanted to send me a package, he had to get Administration's permission. If he wanted to leave any money while visiting me or mail me any money or leave me a package while visiting me, he had to get Administration's permission.

If he mailed me a package without Administration's permission, I would be given a misbehavior report for soliciting to the public. What a shame that my own brother wasn't allowed to send me anything without permission. But I was glad he was coming and that he would be bringing me some things I needed to survive in this so-called prison life. I was still in denial because I kept telling myself that I was getting out when the Appellate Court heard my case. I was still trying to hold on to the little faith I had in the criminal justice system.

Every time I went into the yard, I saw the Muslims. They were always doing something together. The unity I saw among them was outstanding because everyone respected them. Even the COs didn't mess with Muslims. Of course, there were always the roughneck COs who didn't care what group you belonged to; they would harass you just because you belonged to a group. Those COs were the troublemakers, the ones who would start riots in the yard and they would put correctional workers' lives in jeopardy. If a bunch of COs jumped a Muslim, there was instant retaliation launched against the COs. The Muslims were the ones who stood up against Administration. They were the ones who controlled the politics of the jail as far as inmates' concerns.

I was so impressed that I started going to their services. Khalil, who was an old-timer, took me to their services. Muslims had their services on Fridays. When I got there, I didn't realize there were so many more Muslims there than I saw in the yard. There must have been four hundred Muslims at services that Friday.

As I continued going to their services, Brother Khalil was like a mentor to me. He taught me the ropes of prison. When I started school, Khalil was in the class next door, which was the carpentry shop. He made all kinds of picture frames that he used to sell to the population. He never charged me. When I left the school without getting my GED because I wanted to work in the plate shop to make more money, Khalil was upset with me. He wanted me in school because he knew how ignorant I was.

I finally committed myself to the Sunni Muslim community. Khalil taught me enough to say I knew a little about them. He taught me how to say the five mandatory prayers. He taught me the five pillars of Islam, and he taught me about the phony people who were into Islam. When

I was going to their services as a guest, the Muslims had chairs placed in the back, but once I became a Muslim, I had to sit on the rug with the rest. They sat in ranks. Usually the services began at 1:00 p.m. on Friday and would be over about three.

I now had to attend the Muslim classes to learn how to pray properly, to learn the history of Islam and how to read the Quran. The older Muslims were on a mission when it came to teaching us young brothers. They taught me how to survive and how to stand up for myself as a younger brother coming into the system. Khalil was like an older brother to me.

I got into a fight with another inmate, and I don't remember what the fight was about, but I got my butt whipped. I had two black eyes, and my face was so swollen that I had to hide it from the CO in order to avoid a misbehavior report for fighting. Although the other inmate won the fight, I fought like my life depended on it. After the fight, we eventually became best friends. He told me that although he won the fight, he respected me because I fought and didn't care if I lost or not. I not only got respect from him, I won the respect from other inmates who lived on the tier.

That butt-whipping was my first loss since being incarcerated. Khalil said he was disappointed with me because I should have spoken to him, and he would have squashed it. I didn't want Khalil to feel like he needed to hold my hand. I wanted to stand on my own two feet.

One night when we were in for the night, I was listening to the news and I heard the newsman talking about my case. There had been a stabbing at Elmira Correctional Facility, and my codefendant Jo Jo was involved. The news reporter was talking about my case in detail, and I thought Jo Jo was just stabbed. When a major stabbing happened at a correctional facility, the administration would transfer all the troublemakers to another facility. After my codefendant was stabbed, Elmira transferred a bunch of inmates to Auburn. I knew a few of them, and they told me that Jo Jo had been murdered. I was told that a Hispanic man stabbed him in the chest, and Administration took too long to get him to a hospital. Later, he died being transferred to the hospital.

I couldn't believe it! Jo Jo didn't last a full year being incarcerated in Elmira. We came upstate in September of 1981. He was murdered around July of 1982. The guys who came to Auburn told me that the administration caught the inmate who stabbed him. Some inmates believed that the administration was liable for Jo Jo's death. Where did the inmate get the knife or shank to murder another inmate? It was the administration's responsibility to search and make sure that no one possessed any contraband within the facility.

I don't know if Jo Jo's family ever pursued or hired a lawyer to look into his death. But I was more determined to protect myself by any means necessary. I knew my life was always in danger because I was surrounded by cop killers, serial killers, drug kingpins, armed robbers, and the rest. You couldn't distinguish one inmate from the other. You were just another inmate as far as the next inmate was concerned. When any type of conflict came about, you didn't know if you were having a confrontation with a cop killer or a serial killer. You just didn't know who you were messing with.

Jo Jo's death made me more conscious of my surroundings. I was definitely scared. I couldn't call home and tell anyone because inmates only got one telephone call every two weeks. No exceptions. If an inmate had an emergency and needed a phone call, he must contact the chaplain's office. On top of that, you only had three tries to get in contact with your family. After the third try, your phone call would be suspended until the next two weeks. Some inmates lost contact with their family for years because of how the administration ran the telephone system.

I personally lost contact with the outside world for months at a time. I did get some visits because Jackie came up to see me when she could. Although I felt that it wasn't as often as I thought she should have come, at least she was coming. My brother Joe came up like clockwork. Every chance he got, he was there. Not only did he come as often as he could, but he also brought with him some goodies too. I was like a kid coming from the visiting room.

Auburn was about nine hours from New York City. The bus that brought the families to Auburn would leave at 10:00 p.m. the day before. The families had to be at the bus at least two hours before the bus departed. The bus would arrive to the facility next morning at approximately 7:00 a.m. The administration wouldn't start calling the inmates for their visit until about nine. Then they had to wait another two hours. When the families and inmates finally got together in the visiting room, the families would be so frustrated and tired from traveling and the poor treatment they received from the officers that they became discouraged from coming. Sometimes an inmate's family stopped coming altogether.

The administration allowed the inmates to spend six hours with their families in the visiting room. All inmates had to sit opposite their visitors. Once the inmate's family came into the facility, their lives were in jeopardy as well because riots occasionally happened in the visiting room. Many times, inmates would sneak weapons into the visiting room. Now and then an inmate felt that if he couldn't get to you, he would at least get to your family. He could scar or cut your family member with a razor across the face. Sometimes a fight would break out in the visiting room because an inmate would be having sex in front of another inmate's mother, kids, grandmothers, it didn't matter. The inmate had no regard for the next family.

Every drug a person could get off the street was smuggled through the visiting room. Yes, drugs were smuggled in through packages as well, but the majority of them came through the visiting room. A smuggler, if he was a man, would stuff the drugs way down in his pants. A woman would put the drugs in her underwear. Once he or she got into the visiting room, he or she would go into the bathroom. The inmate would go to the bathroom to retrieve the drugs and put them into his pocket or in his boxers. The exchange of drugs would depend on how the COs were situated in the visiting room.

The majority of the COs didn't like working in the visiting room because after the visit was over, it was their responsibility to search each inmate. This meant the CO had to look up each inmate's butt and under his balls. Because many of the COs didn't like that part of the job, they would let the inmates go through without searching them. Many of the inmates knew which COs didn't like looking at their nuts. I remember one CO who would like looking at the inmates. He would tell the inmates to bend over three or four times.

Once the inmate received the drugs, he would do either of two things: he would slam the drugs into his butt or try his luck with the COs who didn't like to search inmates. Most of the time inmates would go with trying to stuff the drugs up their butts.

There was always drama going on at this prison. Remember, some of the inmates there weren't doing a lot of time. Some were there because they got kicked out of a minimum prison for a variety of reasons. I remember one young inmate about eighteen years old who was working in the mess hall. It was a Sunday when the facility served chicken for lunch. After we had finished eating, two inmates were fighting over a piece of leftover chicken. This young inmate got between the two who were fighting. One of them took out a shank and tried to stab the other inmate, but he missed and stabbed the young inmate in the chest instead. Later, we found out that the young inmate had died from that wound. But even sadder, he was scheduled to go home the following week. It was sad because he didn't belong in a maximum-security prison in the first place when he was only doing a two-to-four-year bid. Of course, the administration locked down the facility for three days following this incident.

As soon as the administration let us out of our cells, a killing took place in the gym. Then approximately three weeks after that, another killing took place in the gym, followed by a shooting in the yard. In this incident, two inmates were going at it with shanks, and the CO was using a bullhorn to tell them to drop their weapons. When they didn't comply, the CO let go a warning shot in the air. With that shot I noticed that a lot of the inmates were lying on the ground. I later asked some of the old-timers what was up with the inmates on the ground. The old-timers told me that when the CO shot in the yard, it was automatic for you to hit the ground because the bullet would sometimes ricochet and would accidently hit somebody. Anyway, the two inmates who were fighting with shanks finally dropped their weapons and lay on the ground at gunpoint until the CO handcuffed and escorted them to SHU.

Prison life was crazy, and everything that was abnormal became normal. Pornography magazines became real girls to some of the inmates. Inmates would masturbate looking at skin flicks, and inmates who borrowed magazines would have to return them in good shape. If the magazines were messed up, a fight or a stabbing would take place. Crazy!

If an inmate got tired of masturbating off of magazines, he would turn to the homosexuals for sexual favors. I know society believes that all inmates engage in homosexuality, but it's far from the truth. The majority were not involved in homosexuality. Yes, the strong brother who you would never think would engage in homosexuality became weak because of the system. I believe that many of these guys who were messing with homosexuals in prison probably started before they were in prison, but they just came out of the closet while they were incarcerated.

I thank the Muslims for keeping me strong because I have never involved myself in any form of homosexuality, although there were some Muslims who were involved in homosexuality on the down low. If one of the brothers found out that a brother was messing with homosexuals, he was sent to protective custody (PC). Otherwise he would be beaten or stabbed. It was that simple. Homosexuality was a violation in the Muslim community.

It wasn't like other groups didn't challenge people. For example, the Five-Percent Nation was a powerful group that the population respected. The Black Liberation Army (BLA) was another group was respected in the population. But to make things real crazy, these groups used to fight against each other to the point of death. I remember when the Muslims and the BLA got into a fight because the two leaders didn't like each other. I was involved with both groups. The BLA was teaching me black history, and we used to meet three times a week in the library.

I didn't understand the situation with the leaders, but there was a riot in the yard between the Muslims and BLA. When the smoke cleared, two Muslim brothers had been killed. And these two men were some good brothers. They were humble and liked to help the younger brothers who were having a hard time adjusting to the system. If someone needed help with their law work, these two brothers would help them without charging anyone. It was a shame those brothers were killed because these two leaders were on some nonsense. Of course, the facility closed down for three days for a major search. The leaders were charged for the death of these two Muslim brothers. I heard that the two leaders had placed a bet on their sentences. They were sentenced to ten years apiece in SHU.

I spent my first six years in that madhouse, Auburn Correctional Facility. My counselor finally asked me if I wanted to be transferred to a lower classification facility. What kind of question was that? Going to a lower classification facility meant that I would be closer to home. I came to Auburn in 1981 and I left in 1987. I came in knowing nothing about prison life, but when I left, I was fully adjusted to the prison system. But my education wasn't any better because I left school to work in the plate shop. My finances were better, but I was a total knucklehead. I fought with someone every time I felt a little disrespected.

Jackie visited me once in a while, but not as much as I would have liked. She would sometimes bring my daughter. Those times when I saw my baby girl were the best. I remember when my baby girl first came to see me when I was in the Brooklyn House of Detention. Taneé was only about thirteen months old and tiny. Every time she came into the visiting room, she would run to me, and I would throw her up in the air. She loved when I did that. She would laugh and ask me to do it again and again.

As the years went by, throwing my baby girl up in the air was replaced by a hug. I was hoping that a transfer to a closer facility would mean that I would see my baby girl a little more. Although I didn't know which jail they were sending me to, it didn't matter because I was happy to get out of Auburn. I thank God I survived that madhouse.

The CO finally told us that we were going to the Eastern Correctional Facility, a maximum B facility. Many inmates called Eastern "Happy Nap." When I got there, I made a conscious decision to pursue my education. Eastern was known to have the best education program within the state prison system. Inmates earned associate, bachelor's, and master's degrees and recreation leadership certificates. I felt that it was really time for me to get myself together and stop all the fighting or else I would wind up being in prison for the rest of my life.

My appeal was denied. The Appellate Division Courts agreed with the lower court. so my conviction was upheld. I didn't know what to do at this point of my life. Once the Appellate Division confirmed my sentence, my recourse as far as me pursuing my innocence was zero because I didn't know anything about the law.

I didn't trust the jailhouse lawyers because they were a bunch of con artists. They would take an inmate's money or his family's money and put something together to submit to the court. The inmate's conviction would be affirmed, and the inmate would find an excuse to not to pay off the jailhouse lawyer. That would cause a serious problem between the two inmates. Many of those jailhouse lawyers got stabbed because they would be messing around with people's cases and sell somebody a dream. So I didn't mess with the jailhouse lawyers.

"Prison is itself a tremendous education in the need for patience and perseverance. It is, above all, a test of one's commitment. Those who passed through that school have all acquired a firmness, tempered by a remarkable resilience."

—Nelson Mandela
February 11, 1994

The Eastern Correction Facility

When I was in Auburn, I found myself getting into trouble all the time. In fact, I fought so much that I was the first inmate who received thirty days in the box for fighting. I was kind of shocked because usually the disciplinary officer gave only seven days for fighting. But that did not deter me, and I ended up doing the same things after being in the box as I had done before.

For instance, when one of the Muslims jumped a CO, I was the one charged with the assault. What happened was that a few days after that incident, I was yelling to a friend who lived on the third tier for him to come to the yard after chow. When the CO was opening the cell doors for us to go to the yard, my door didn't open. I yelled for the CO to open my cell door, thinking he'd forgotten. When the CO made his rounds, I asked him why he hadn't opened my cell door, and he told me that I was on lockdown. I asked him why, but he didn't answer me.

I asked someone who was going to the yard to tell Brother Nahim to come see me to find out why I was being locked in. Brother Nahim was the inmate liaison representative. He told me that the partner of the CO who was assaulted was working on the tier above mine at the time of the assault, and he said that I was the one who beat up the CO because he recognized my voice. I was shocked when I heard that. Then Brother Nahim said that when I yelled to my friend that day, the CO identified my voice.

When I went before the court, the judge asked the C.O., "What is your occupation?"

He replied, "I'm a corrections officer."

The judge then asked, "Are you a voice expert?" He admitted he wasn't. The judge then asked how he could distinguish Mr. Murray's voice from the rest of the population of 2800 inmates. This idiot informed the judge that he just could. The judge immediately dismissed the charges, but the facility gave me five years in the box because I had violated the facility's rules and regulations.

I asked the disciplinary officer how the judge could dismiss the case but the facility still penalize me. He just said that the court had nothing to do with the facility's rules and regulations. I spent thirteen months in the box before the court ordered my release. God forbid if I had been convicted for assaulting the CO! It would have been more time added to the time I was already doing. Very scary! So I really made the decision to get myself together before I spent the rest of my life in prison.

When I finally went to program committee, I knew what I wanted. They gave me a pre-GED class and commercial art classes which included subjects like general accounting. I breezed through the pre-GED class and was transferred to the regular GED class. Ms. Jackson taught the GED class. She was a very concerned black lady, and everybody liked her. Some of the teachers were worse than the COs, although racism wasn't as strong at the Eastern Correctional Facility as it was in Auburn. Yes, there were plenty of black COs working at the facility, but the white ones were as racist as those in Auburn.

Ms. Jackson was like a mother to all the inmates. She really gave me individual help because she saw my determination to get my GED. When the pretest came up, I passed with flying colors. Ms. Jackson was so proud of us who passed the test that she brought in a cake. When the GED test came around, I studied real hard because I wanted to pass the test the first time. Therefore, when the population went into the yard, I stayed in my cell studying. I sacrificed about a month without going to the yard, but it definitely paid off, because I passed the test.

When I started college classes, one of the classes was public speaking. I had to go before inmates and talk about a familiar topic. I didn't have the slightest idea what I was going to talk about. My professor came up with a perfect idea. He told me to speak about myself. When I went before the class, I was scared to death. I could barely remember my name. I kept stuttering to the point that the professor told me to have a seat. As the weeks went on, I got much better at controlling my fear. In fact, I got a B-plus in that class.

I started running for a political office within the facility. I became the vice president of the Break Thru in Art (BTIA). The president was this inmate named Snake. One day Snake got locked down for smoking weed, and the administration gave him four months in the box. When Snake came out of the box, he tried getting his position as president back, but I wouldn't go for it because not only did he violate the rules and regulations of the facility, he also violated the by-laws of the organization. When I told him he couldn't get the presidency back, he started a rumor that I was telling the administration on him. Remember, I came from an environment where there was zero tolerance among inmates for snitching. Therefore, many waited to see if I would handle my business.

Since I was Muslim, I couldn't make a move without the Imam's approval. When I presented my case to the Imam, he asked me what I wanted to do. I told him that I wanted to fight him. Some of the brothers wanted to stab him, but it wasn't that serious. Once the Imam gave me permission, Brother Latif and Brother Umar came with me to make sure no one jumped on me.

As soon as I saw Snake in the yard, I jumped on him, and the next thing I knew, Brothers Latif and Umar were pulling me off of him. I must have lost it because I didn't remember anything. Umar and Latif told me later that I was stomping Snake out, and if they hadn't stopped me, I would have hurt him badly.

Three days after the fight, two COs and a sergeant came into the yard and told me to put my hands in my pockets. Anytime the CO told an inmate to put his hands in his pockets, that meant that he was being locked in. They escorted me to my cell and told me I was being locked in for fighting. I couldn't believe it because it was a whole three days after the incident. Some suspected it was Snake who told the sergeant because he felt so bad after getting his butt beaten. Snake wanted to leave the facility. When I went before the adjustment committee, the disciplinary officer dismissed the fighting charge because no one came to testify that I was fighting. Snake went into protective custody (PC), and eventually he left the facility. I continued being the president of the BTIA.

I joined the Inmate Liaison Committee (ILC) and gave my first argument in front of the administration on behalf of the inmates who lived in B3. I did so poorly that the ILC president had to come to my aid. He told me not to worry about my mistakes because he would help me become better. When I gave my second argument, I did a somewhat better presentation. I wasn't as sharp as the other representatives, but I was improving as I went along.

One of my big problems was getting too emotional and argumentative when presenting my arguments. The ILC president kept telling me to take my time when I was speaking. I needed to tone myself down because I was demanding as opposed to requesting. I started presenting my arguments with a much calmer attitude. As a result, I started winning decisions.

My adjustment in Eastern Correctional Facility was doing me some good because I wasn't getting into a lot of trouble. I only had one fight since being at Happy Nap. I was getting more visits from my little brother Joe. Even when he moved to Georgia, he would come see me whenever he made the trip to visit the family, and he brought me packages. When I didn't call, he would call the facility and talk to my counselor to find out if I was okay. Every time I failed to call, he would be on that phone calling the facility.

In 1988, the facility established a kid's playroom within the visiting room because kids were running around in there. The facility got sued because one of the kids fell and hit his head on the corner of a table. The parents sued the facility. As a result, the administration created a playroom. I was recommended by the superintendent to be interviewed for the caretaker's job in the visiting room. Once I was approved, I had to take a parenting class for me to become a caretaker. Once I finished the parenting class and passed, I was assigned as a volunteer to work in the visiting room. I was the first one with a murder conviction who worked in the visiting room.

I remember every time I came into the visiting room, the kids would run right to me, and I developed a relationship with them. The kids' fathers used to get upset with me because their kids would literally run out of their parents' arms to come to me. I used to tell the inmates they should come into the kids' room so that they could interact with them, but they never came into the playroom because they were too preoccupied with trying to have sex with their kid's mother. I was their babysitter for the six hours they were in the visiting room. It was crazy because they were more concerned with interacting with the mother instead of trying to establish a relationship with their own kids. Many of the inmates really didn't want to see their kids. They used their kids as an excuse so that their girlfriends would come to see them.

I remember once when the whole facility came down with diarrhea because the water got affected by a beaver who crapped into the reservoir. All the inmates came down with a parasite called "beaver fever." The nurses were frustrated because they were forced by the administration to take samples of each inmate in the facility. The deputy of security told the nurses that we couldn't take the tube back to our cell because it contained a dangerous chemical. Those nurses were crying because the facility had a population of about 1800 inmates.

All the water was cut off, and water was brought into the facility. Life was very hectic in the facility without access to water. Only at night did the facility turn on the water so we could flush the toilets. The whole facility smelled foul. But we had no choice but to live through it as opposed to the COs, who wore masks and went home after eight hours. We were like animals to the administration. They didn't care that the whole situation was a health problem. Our lives didn't mean much. We were just a bunch of convicted criminals.

I graduated college in 1990 and got kicked out of Happy Nap because of some crazy nonsense that another inmate did. The Jay-Cee Festival was usually one of the best family festivals. At one of these festivals, one of the inmates started dancing on an American flag. The next thing I knew, I saw all these people dancing on the flag. The COs didn't try to stop them. They just stood there like everything was all right. Usually, if some strange incident happened, the CO would approach the inmate and give him a warning. If the behavior continued, then the inmate was escorted out of the festival. But apparently the administration was offended. I didn't understand why the whole committee was being punished because of one inmate who started the incident. The administration decided to transfer the entire committee. They divided about thirty of us into four prisons. We didn't know where we were going until the day of the transfer. The next thing I knew was that I was being searched, my feet were being shackled, chains were wrapped around my waist, and my hands were being cuffed. I was headed to the Attica Correctional Facility.

Attica Correctional Facility

I was really intimidated about Attica because the only thing I knew about the facility was the famous riot in 1971 where a bunch of inmates and COs were killed during the uprising. When my group got to Attica, we were escorted to the reception block where we were searched again. The COs were giants compared to the ones in Auburn and Eastern Corrections. Immediately you could tell that they were more racist than two facilities I'd been in. They had us stand against the wall, and we weren't allowed to speak unless we were spoken to.

The COs' orientation was totally an intimidation tactic. They got up in our faces and dared us to say anything. They weren't playing games. One inmate who was on the bus with me gave the CO a hard time, and the next thing I saw was that inmate lying on the floor. The COs were kicking and punching him. They were using him as an example to teach us what we could expect if we got out of line.

When the COs escorted us to D Block, they had us in twos. The CO explained to us that when he knocked on the wall with his nightstick once, it meant to stop. When he hit the wall twice, it meant to proceed. If anyone disobeyed orders, one of two things could happen: (1) the CO could give him a misbehavior report, or (2) the COs could jump him and make an example of him in front of the other inmates. Usually the second one happened.

Attica was a controlled environment prison. I guess they didn't want another riot. It was one of the worst riots in prison history. Attica is surrounded by a thirty-foot wall two feet thick, with fourteen gun towers. At the time of the riot, 54 percent of the inmates were black, and all of the guards were white, many of them openly racist. Prisoners spent fourteen to sixteen hours a day in their cells. Their mail was read; their reading material was restricted; their visits from families took place through a mesh screen; the parole system was inequitable. When prisoners were up for parole, the average duration of their hearing, including the reading of the file and deliberation among the three-member board, was five minutes. The board's decision was handed down with no explanation.

On September 9, 1971, a series of conflicts between prisoners and guards ended with a relatively minor incident, involving a guard disciplining two prisoners. This was the spark that set off the revolt when a group of inmates from D Block broke through a gate and took over one of the four prison yards with forty guards as hostages. After five days, the state lost patience. Governor Nelson Rockefeller approved a military attack on the prison. One thousand national guardsmen, prison guards, and local police went in with automatic rifles and submachine guns in a full-scale assault on the prisoners, who had no firearms. Thirty-one prisoners were killed. The first stories given the press by prison authorities said the nine guards held hostage had their throats slashed by the prisoners during the attack. The official autopsies almost immediately showed this to be false. Nine guards died in the same hail of bullets that killed the prisoners.

When I came upstate, the Attica riot was still in the air at all the state correctional facilities. Even some the COs were transferred to prisons elsewhere in the state. One CO who worked in Auburn was actually saved by one of the prisoners in Attica because most of the inmates there liked him. Generally, he treated the prisoners fairly. This

CO worked in Auburn's plate shop, and again most of the inmates still liked him. When I had the opportunity to speak with him, he was one of the nicest people you ever met. He didn't like speaking about his experience during the riot.

The COs definitely controlled the entire facility. Attica was divided into cell blocks, and each block had its own recreation yard. The only time you would see another inmate from another cell block was at program. I only stayed at Attica for about a year and I was glad to get out of there because the COs were the worst as far as jumping on an inmate. They would kill you and then justify the murder. I had been incarcerated for almost ten years now, and I had never heard of a CO losing a case for murdering an inmate. It was crazy there. Thank God I was transferred back to Auburn Correctional Facility.

Second Time in Auburn

When I got back in Auburn, the facility had changed. The younger generation had a totally different concept of respecting each other. I guess it was because of the gangs in prison. I'm speaking about the Bloods, Crips, Latin Kings, and a few other gangs trying to make a name for themselves. These younger inmates were slicing each other's faces with razors for stupid reasons. The gangs were so out of control that the administration started separating recreation between the blocks. When I first came to Auburn in 1981, all the blocks went to rec together except at night.

When I returned to Auburn, I heard that there had been a riot between the Jamaicans and the Latinos over drugs. Drugs were a major problem within the facility because there was a lot of money involved. Although there were drugs when I first came to Auburn in 1981, there were more drugs now, and each gang tried to get control over it.

There were four evils in prison and if an inmate could stay away from those evils, he should be all right. (But again, the catch-22 was always in effect: act crazy, or become a victim.) The four evils were drugs, gangs, gambling, and homosexuality. Sometimes inmates would buy drugs on credit and couldn't pay the dealer, who then had no choice but to make an example of the inmate. Everyone was looking to see if the drug dealer was going to make a move on that person. If the drug dealer didn't make a move on him, no one who owed the drug dealer would pay him because they saw his weakness. It meant that the drug dealer was soft.

The second evil was gangs. The reason why gangs became an evil was because the members were always at risk for their lives or getting cut across the face with a razor. Members didn't really have to do anything, because if a member from another group was violated, he wasn't going to find the other gang member who violated him. He would settle for revenge against any member of the other group.

The next evil was gambling. When individuals gambled, they usually exceeded the amount they could afford. When they couldn't pay their debt, their lives were in jeopardy. If the person who was due money didn't make a move, he would be seen as soft.

The last but not least evil was homosexuality. Two inmates were always fighting over someone for homosexual favors. When the smoke cleared, the two inmates would be gone, but the homosexual would be the only one left standing. One fighter likely went to the box and the other to the hospital.

Auburn was totally out of control with stabbings and slicing each other with razors. The old-timers who taught brothers like me were now scared of the younger generation. The old-timers didn't want to be bothered because they were afraid that the younger brother would turn on them.

My life in prison was now totally different than when I first came to prison. I'd been in prison for over thirteen years at this point. Although I was still very angry, I was now placing myself around good brothers who were into education. I had my associate's degree, and I was working in the prerelease center. I was now helping inmates prepare to leave prison. If an inmate didn't have his birth certificate or Social Security card or needed a residence or possible employment, it was my responsibility to assist him in obtaining the required documents before going to the parole board.

Although the parole board required every inmate to have these documents, I heard stories about how the board was hitting inmates for the least thing. One inmate I helped was making his third appearance before the parole board. He told me that the parole board kept hitting him for the nature of the crime. He was incarcerated for murder and the judge sentenced him to fifteen-to-life. He had been incarcerated for nineteen years for the same crime. The parole board kept telling him that, because of the nature of the crime, they kept giving him an additional two years.

I had only two more years before I was eligible for parole. The stories I was hearing about the parole board were very discouraging, but I felt confident that once I told my story, they would parole me. So I felt these stories didn't affect me.

I worked in the prerelease center up until I was transferred to a lower classification facility. Right before I was transferred, there was a shooting in the yard. Two inmates were fighting with shanks, and when the warning shot came, everyone instinctively hit the ground except those who didn't know any better. The two inmates who were fighting disregarded the warning shot, and the next thing I knew, one of them was hit with a bullet and fell to the ground.

The COs came running and handcuffed both inmates. I was amazed that they restrained the inmate who was shot. Why do that? Wasn't it enough that he was on the ground bleeding and screaming? The COs roughed up both inmates while they were containing them. It my experience that those COs took every opportunity to rough up inmates, no matter what.

After they escorted one of the inmates to the hospital and the other to the box, they closed the yard. We were once again in our cells for three days with no shower, no hot food, and no programs while the facility conducted a major search.

After we were let out of our cells, the CO informed me that I had to see my counselor. After I took my shower, I proceeded to see my counselor, who informed me I was going to be transferred to a lower classification facility. I was glad when he told me that my case was reversed from when I was kicked out of Eastern Correctional Facility because another inmate decided to dance on the American flag. My counselor told me that the facility had messed up because there wasn't any report to justify transferring me out of the facility. Therefore, since my behavior at Eastern was basically good, Albany decided to transfer me to a lower classification facility. I was happy that I was getting out of Auburn.

*"To be alone in prison is a difficulty.
You must never try it."*

*—Nelson Mandela
April 6, 1993*

ONEIDA CORRECTIONAL FACILITY

I was transferred to Oneida Correctional Facility in 1992, located in Rome, New York. The population was about 1200 inmates, housed in a dormitory setting. After we were searched, the C.O.s took us to a dormitory that housed about sixty inmates. I immediately didn't like this setting because I was used to being in a cell.

I knew from the beginning that I wasn't going to remain in this facility. I just didn't know how I was going to pull it off without getting myself into trouble. The inmates were running around like they didn't have a problem in the world. They were very relaxed.

The facility ran their recreation every hour on the hour. The only thing you had to do when you went to the yard was to sign the recreation sheet so that the CO knew where you were. The only thing we did in the maximum was walk around the yard in a circle. In Oneida, it was like a college campus. I saw people and cars going by when I was in the yard. I was scared to walk near the gate because in the maximum, you couldn't go near an exit gate, or else you went to the box immediately.

The dormitory had three washing machines, three dryers, a stove, a refrigerator, pots and pans, and a TV area. It was definitely a relaxed environment, but at the same time, it was a dangerous environment. When I was in a maximum, the only people who had access to me when I was in my cell were the COs. But at Oneida, the dormitory was divided into sixty cubicles. The cubicle was just big enough for a bed and a locker. The inmate in the next cubicle could just stand up and look straight down on the next person while he slept. As a result, anyone could attack you while you were sleeping. I wanted out. I wanted to go back to a maximum prison where I felt more comfortable. I spoke to my counselor about going back to a max, but he told me that I couldn't unless I got into trouble.

When I went to the program committee, they assigned me as a teacher's aide in the pre-GED class. Although I liked being a teacher's aide, it was a challenge when a person didn't want any help. The only reason several inmates were in school was because it was mandated by the administration and the parole board. So many inmates were just going through the motions of getting promoted to the next level. Only a few were promoted at a time, but the majority of the inmates were left back. I knew a few inmates who were in pre-GED class for many years because they gave up on education.

At first it was hard being a teacher's aide, but after getting familiar with the younger generation of inmates, I realized that many were just fronting because they didn't know how to read and write. After becoming familiar with me, many of them started asking me to help them write letters to their families, friends, and girlfriends. One inmate who was in the class and also lived in my dormitory came to ask me for some advice about a situation he was going through. He was going home the following week, but one of the gang leaders wanted him to make a hit on another inmate. The only advice I could give him was to sign himself into PC. He didn't want to sign himself in, and he didn't want to do the assignment that the leader had given him. He figured he would stay in the dormitory until he went home.

But the gang leader sent a couple of inmates to the dormitory with razors and started slicing the inmate who was going home. I had never seen so much blood coming out of anyone. Blood was all over the place. The two inmates were caught, of course.

I remember another incident when an inmate was working as the laundry man, washing inmates' clothes. One inmate got into an argument with the laundry man for putting his clothes in the washing machine. The argument got so far out of control that the laundry man took it personally. He waited until everyone was asleep, brought some cooking oil to a boil, and poured in in the face of the inmate who had argued with him.

It was four o'clock in the morning when I heard a very loud scream and jumped out of bed to see where the noise was coming from. I couldn't believe what I saw. This man's skin was literally peeling off his face. Unbelievable! After that incident, I really wanted out of that jail. I spoke to my counselor again about transferring to another jail, and he told me to keep my nose clean until after my first parole board appearance.

First Parole Board Appearance

I was still in Oneida Correctional Facility and about nine months away from my first parole board appearance. I still didn't like this jail because a lot of young inmates there were acting crazy. I was having a problem with one old-timer who had enticed a young boy to go into my cubicle and steal my boots.

I was in the yard working out when it happened. When I came back from the yard, one of the guys told me that a young inmate had stolen my boots. When I confronted him, he just told me to get out of his face. I tried not to allow him to take me out of character, but when I asked him a third time, he punched me in the face. So I went to my cube and got my net bag and put three cans in it and proceeded to teach this guy a lesson to not mess with people's stuff.

The young boy went to the hospital. He didn't tell Administration on me. But another inmate told the sergeant, and then two COs and a sergeant came to my cube and told me to put my hands in my pockets. They handcuffed me and then escorted me down the corridor to the box. They didn't say a word the whole time. They took me to the strip room and told me to take everything off, so that they could look into every orifice for drugs and weapons. Then they escorted me to a cell. I was going to be in that cell for twenty-three hours a day, with one hour of recreation time in a cage. Three ten-minute showers a week, on Monday, Wednesday, and Friday.

When I went to the adjustment committee, a captain held the hearing. He informed me after his investigation that he was well aware of what had happened, because snitchers told him the whole story. He said I should have told someone before I went off. He sentenced me to six months in the box.

The governor of New York had special housing units built throughout the state, called S Block. These special housing units were built primarily for inmates who were involved in gang-related infractions. I couldn't believe how things were run in Oneida's S Block. First they took me into a search cell and searched my whole body. Then they gave me one pair of green pants, a green shirt, a pair of underwear, an undershirt, a pair of socks, a pair of state boots, five magazines, and five books. This was the only property I could have while in the box.

When I was informed that I would be in the cell with another inmate, I lost my mind. The cell had bunk beds, a toilet, a small sink, a shower, two desks built into the wall, and a sliding door in the back of the cell so that we would have our recreation. It was crazy. The rec area only consisted of walking about five steps the long way and I could extend my arms for the width between the wall and the gate.

If the inmates couldn't get along with each other and a fight broke out, the CO couldn't open the cell door unless his immediate supervisor was present. The sergeant could be anywhere in the facility doing something else. In the meantime, the inmates would be fighting. Some inmates were beaten up, raped, or even murdered because no one came to their rescue of the inmate fast enough. What was really crazy was the administration would put two inmates from different gangs, let's say a Blood and a Latin King, in the same cell, knowing that they were enemies. Subsequently, one of the inmates would be murdered.

When I was placed in S Block, they put me in a cell with a man who had mental problems. He was even getting medication for his illness. Sometimes I would wake up in the middle of the night and this guy would be standing over me while I was sleeping. It became so bad, I asked to be taken out of the cell and put in another cell with someone who wasn't crazy. The sergeant understood my plight and told me he had the right inmate to put with me.

Being in that box was my worst time since I had been incarcerated. I was only within a few months of my first parole board appearance, and being in the box would not look good. But I wasn't sweating it because stuff just happens while being in jail. One major thing that I learned from that experience was not to let anyone get you out of control to where you could harm yourself or someone else.

When I went before my first parole board, it was in June 1994. There were three commissioners sitting behind a desk shuffling through papers when I came in. The commissioner in the middle told me to sit down. He asked me to state my name and number. After he asked me some basic questions for the record. Then the commissioner said that I was still violent, and they would see me in twenty-four months.

I was mad. They didn't ask me anything about the case besides reading what was on record. They told me I was still violent. Who were they talking about? They couldn't have been talking about me because I was in there for something I didn't do. I didn't have a chance to even explain myself.

They didn't ask me anything about what I learned while being incarcerated. During my incarceration, I earned my high school diploma. I completed a general business course receiving a certificate for typing more than forty words a minute. I also earned a few certificates of merit for being a teacher's aide. Furthermore, I had completed several job training courses. I had also been active in volunteer work while in prison and received numerous certificates of appreciation for my efforts. I was sure that I would be paroled. How could they hold me responsible for fighting in an abnormal environment? Didn't they know I was surrounded by the worst criminals in the state of New York?

In the time that I had been incarcerated during these fifteen years, I saw hundreds of inmates who were either stabbed, sliced across their faces, jumped by other inmates or murdered by a CO or an inmate. Some may think that I shouldn't have assaulted that young man because of some boots. But it wasn't about the boots. It was the principle that if I had left it alone, it would have happened to me over and over again. In prison, you couldn't afford anyone taking advantage of you. Only the strong survived in that kind of environment. I saw it hundreds of times when an inmate didn't want to deal with the situation the prison way and got taken advantage of during his incarceration. I could have dealt with the situation differently. I gave the parole board ammunition to use against me because of a knucklehead who was influenced by an old-timer who couldn't stand on his own two feet. Yes, my way of thinking was based on prison life. Fifteen years was more than half my life! Although at this point I had more education, I still lashed out at anyone who was a threat to me.

I don't remember exactly when, but the chaplain called me down to his office to inform me that my sister had called to notify me that my brother had died. It was my brother Anthony, the one Jo Jo said he was with on the day of the murder. I couldn't believe it. The chaplain asked me if I wanted to go to his wake, but I wouldn't be allowed to attend the funeral. Of course I wanted to go to the wake. This was an opportunity to see my family, and I hadn't seen some of them in years.

The COs took me to the state shop to fit me into some clothes and then transported me to the wake in Manhattan. Right before I went into the funeral parlor, the COs informed me that they would allow me three hours to grieve with my family members. They told me that they would take off the chains around my waist and the handcuffs, but the feet shackles must stay on during the entire wake. The shackles didn't matter to me because I was seeing my family.

While I was sitting in the van, one of my nieces saw me and ran to tell my daughter I was outside. I saw my daughter running toward the van, but I couldn't get out and hug her, nor could she come inside the van to give me a hug. The COs were apprehensive because they knew from my file that I had a big family. Within a mile of the funeral parlor the COs contacted the local precinct to inform them that a convict was in the neighborhood.

A lot of people were inside the funeral parlor. Once I was inside, my daughter came running into my arms and gave me a big hug. All my family followed and gave me hugs. They told me that Anthony had been arrested for robbery and that he was convicted and went upstate to do a three-and-a-half to nine–year bid. Only a few months into his bid, he came down with an illness that knocked him down. He was diagnosed with HIV which resulted in AIDS. The disease came down on him so hard that he passed away within weeks after he was diagnosed.

Sitting and looking at my brother in the casket, I was thinking that all who were allegedly involved in the murder were dead. Jo Jo died within a year of going upstate, and my brother died within a year of being incarcerated. Was God telling me something? I still was very angry although I controlled the anger at this point of my incarceration.

I was truly scared of dying in prison. Since I been in prison so many people died: my sister Darlene, my favorite Aunt Bobby, my father, my cousin Bubble, and many more. Yes, dying in prison was my biggest fear, so I really went out of my way to protect myself. When I received the board's decision I knew right away that I could not give them any more ammunition to use against me when I went before them again.

Their official decision was that "because of the seriousness of the nature of the crime with your disciplinary record, we the parole board do not see fit to parole you without you staying at liberty in society." To me it was a crazy decision because the nature of the crime would never change. It would not matter if the crime was committed a hundred years ago. I understood the crime was serious and that an innocent man should not have been murdered. For many years I could not talk about the crime because I was too embarrassed. But I wasn't the one who committed the murder. My innocence wasn't even considered.

I believe I was in that room no more than three minutes. It took me two days to receive a hard copy of the decision. Waiting for the parole board's decision was the worst mental pressure that you could ever imagine. Although I knew the decision verbally, I was still hoping that they would let me go. Maybe they went over the case and they were trying to scare me before they let me go. I'd heard stories that the parole board screamed at inmates but in writing let them go home. Usually, when the parole board let those inmates out, they knew they would be back into the system. The revolving door was out of control as far as inmates coming back and forth to prison multiple times in their life. It was like a second home to many of them. As soon as they came back to prison, they would reconnect with the same individuals they'd left behind. It was as if the person never left the system.

The parole board gave me two additional years in prison. I was no longer doing the minimum of the sentence that the judge gave me. I was doing life in prison. The next time I would see the parole board, I would have spent seventeen years in prison.

That night when the CO turned off the lights, I cried like a baby. It didn't make any sense to me because I had already done the minimum sentence for a crime I didn't commit. Why was I still being punished? The system was failing me and I was losing faith. I cried and cried and cried.

The administration finally let me out the box for good behavior. I did only four months out of the six, which was a blessing. No one should have to suffer and go into a place like that. It was definitely inhumane for any person. The food was rationed more so than for the general population. Usually when someone went into the box, he would come out fifteen or twenty pounds thinner. The medical department didn't treat you like the inmates in population either.

The administration then moved me to Fishkill Correctional Facility which was another medium facility. I thought they would send me back to a maximum facility. I was glad when CO told me I was going to Fishkill because I didn't want to go back into a maximum facility.

Fishkill Correctional Facility

It was 1994 when I got to Fishkill Correctional Facility. Fishkill was a medium/maximum facility. I was actually surprised that the administration had sent me to a facility so close to the city. I had decided not to let the parole board's decision get me down any longer. Many nights when those lights went out, I cried. I was hurting inside. I couldn't see any light in the tunnel, but every time the flame would almost be out, a little light would show up telling me that everything would be all right.

My biggest source of hope came from my innocence and my daughter. I had to stay strong for my daughter because I didn't want her to see me in a weak state. It took me some time before I finally told her I wasn't coming home. She was now sixteen years old, and her hope of my coming home was high. It took me about two weeks after I received the decision to inform her that I wasn't coming home.

When I told her over the phone, she got really quiet. I kept calling her name, but she didn't say a word. When she finally spoke, I heard the disappointment in her voice, and I asked her if she was all right. She said yes, but I still heard the pain in her voice. I felt like I'd failed her again. Her hope of my return home was up really high prior to my parole board hearing. Although I tried to prepare her for the possibility of my not coming home, she just believed that the parole board was going to release me. The only thing I could tell her was that they would let me go the next time.

Fishkill had cells and dormitories. There were two sides of the facility: down the hill and up the hill. Inmates who lived up the hill were in a dormitory which was called Building 21. Inmates who lived down the hill were in cells in what was considered the main building. After the CO had strip-searched me for drugs and weapons, they took me to Building 21. I was surprised that the administration housed me with inmates who were living in the dormitories. I had just come out of four months in the box for attacking another inmate. Now, the administration placed me in another dormitory. Amazing! I made up my mind not to let anyone take me out of character unless it was a life-and-death situation.

I was housed in K Unit, where there were approximately sixty inmates. There was one TV, four telephones, two hot plates to cook on, four showers, and about six toilets for all sixty inmates. When the CO assigned me to my cube, it had only a bunk bed and a locker. The CO had sent me there with a change of linens, a tube of toothpaste, a toothbrush, and a bar of soap. I wasn't allowed to have any of my personal property until it was searched by the Property CO. I would receive my belongings in three or four days. Although I had personal property from another jail, that didn't mean those items would automatically be allowed in here. In fact, most of my things weren't allowed in Fishkill Correctional Facility.

After I got settled, I went out to the yard, where I saw many familiar faces from Eastern and Auburn. There were several guys that I started out with there and gotten to know, although I wasn't tight with any of them. Many of them were Muslim too. I had left the Muslim community since I got kicked out of Eastern Correctional in the late eighties and early nineties. Since then, I had decided to turn my life over to Christ.

When I was in Eastern, a Christian brother invited me to a Sunday service because a gospel group came into the facility to perform. Being Muslim, I wasn't allowed to clap when I heard something that excited me. We Muslims were taught to say, "Allahuakbar," which meant "Allah is the Greatest." When I heard the gospel singers, it really stirred something inside of me. I wanted to clap, I wanted to shout, and it was making me feel good. I wanted some of that glow I saw in the Christian brothers. It was a glow that let everyone else know they were blessed.

I had never felt that way when I was a part of the Muslim community. I didn't feel any spiritual emotion the entire time I was a part of the Muslim community. I just became part of them because I appreciated their unity. I appreciated the older Muslim brothers who taught me how to stand on my own two feet. Brothers like Khalil taught me how to be a man. But as far as any spiritual connection, I wasn't feeling anything. I'm not saying that the other brothers weren't spiritual. Khalil, for example, was a very spiritual brother, and all the brothers respected him.

When Sunday came, the first thing I did was attend Protestant services. After Reverend Boston delivered his sermon, he asked if anyone wanted to give their life to the Lord. I was a little hesitant, but eventually I submitted my life to Christ. It felt good because it was a good service that day. Reverend Boston asked me to repeat the words of commitment to Christ, and after that the congregation of Christian brothers came over to me and gave me a hug. I felt really good at that point in my life.

The pastor told me that I had to work on becoming Christlike. He told me that even though I was getting baptized the following week, just coming out of the water didn't mean that I would be holy. It only meant that it was a new beginning to my spiritual life. I must bring about a Christlike attitude.

It was a new beginning for me. I had just been hit at the parole board, I was fresh out of four months in the box for attacking an inmate, and I was having problems with a younger Muslim who felt I had abandoned the Muslim community. So mentally I had to change my way of thinking. There was no such thing as being part of a Christian gang. Many Christians were physically and verbally abused because they didn't want any problems. They would just take the abuse to show what good Christians they were. But not every Christian brother had reached that level of spirituality to turn the other cheek.

I became part of the choir within a month after I submitted my life to the Lord. Our choir was really good. In fact, it was the reason why I joined the choir because they had sung up a storm every time they sang. Our choir director, Julius Walker, was a perfectionist. He was very good, but he used to get on us so hard that there were a lot of complaints to the pastor about his verbal abuse. He was one of the Christians who didn't take any mess from anybody, not even the COs. The inmates thought he was bugging out because he was always arguing and fighting with someone. Julius was just upset with the system because he had appeared before the parole board at least three times and kept getting an additional two years each time. He had been incarcerated for about twenty years.

When I went to the program committee, they assigned me as a teacher's aide in the GED class. I didn't mind being a teacher's aide because I enjoyed helping the guys out. Some of the inmates knew that I'd just gotten out the box because they heard what had happened in Oneida. But being around familiar faces helped me make a smooth transition from being segregated from the population for four months, especially after the news that I would have to do an additional two years.

Fishkill was a laid-back facility. It was close to the city. It had good programs, and it had a variety of organizations to assist inmates. It had all types of festivals so that families could be with their loved ones and aid in their rehabilitation. Family Day was one of the best times at Fishkill because the administration allowed the inmates to spend up to six hours with their families.

Various organizations would host Family Day. Inmates purchased food for their family members. There was a DJ who played music. Sometimes the organization would have dance contests for the kids and the adults. Sometimes the winner would win money: $25, $50, $100, and even $150. The organization would sponsor all the activities with money raised throughout the year at different fund-raisers so that inmates and their families could enjoy each other's company.

It was really cool, and I definitely took advantage of those times. Joe, my little brother, went to many of those festivals. It didn't matter which jail I was in; he made it his business to come check me out. Many times he would bring my daughter. Those were the good old times even though I was locked up. I remember many times that I had to make special requests to have additional visitors: Joe, Jamal (Joe's son), Kathy (my sister), Lamar (Kathy's son), and Taneé would come to visit me.

My daughter had some good times at those festivals. One time I presented Taneé with a certificate for being a great daughter. She was so embarrassed. But I did it because she was a great daughter, and that was my way of telling her I loved her. Later on during that particular festival she told me that I was a cool dad. That statement made me feel great, and I will never forget it.

My daughter was my lifeline. She was the main reason I knew I had to stay strong. I will always appreciate that her mother made sure that she knew me as her father although we weren't together as a couple. Jackie accepted many collect telephone calls for many, many years so that I could have some form of communication with my daughter.

When my daughter turned sixteen, the administration allowed her to visit by herself with a permission letter from her mother. She didn't come alone too often. She would come mainly with either Joe or her cousin Tracy. They came to see me quite often when I was in Fishkill.

Although Fishkill was laid back, incidents still happened like inmates getting stabbed or cut across their faces and COs jumping on inmates. I became so familiar with the younger inmates that they used to protect me whenever I got into an argument with someone. They would want to fight for me because they didn't want me to get into trouble. They knew I had over fifteen years in prison and that the parole board had just hit me with an additional two years. So they used to ask me if I wanted them to jump on someone. I would tell them no because I didn't want them to get into any trouble themselves.

Three young inmates liked to work out with me. I had rules if they wanted to work out. You couldn't say any curse words. If you were caught using those words, you had to do fifty push-ups. If you didn't do the push-ups, you couldn't work out with us. It was cool because it was like how the older brothers taught me.

After being in the facility for about a year, I was recommended for the Youth Assistance Program (YAP) by the teacher I was working for. I was interviewed by the captain, the YAP coordinator, a CO who assisted the director, and the YAP director. They told me that I was highly recommended and that they were going to assign me to the YAP team, which was made up of twelve inmates. All of them welcomed me to the team as we prepared for a seminar. I was given an educational skit and was told to memorize it. Kids were coming from schools, probation departments, police departments, youth programs, and other departments that sponsor the kid's programs.

YAP emerged from the Scared Straight program that came out of Rahway State Prison. The director of this program did not believe that fear should be used to educate the youth. Therefore, the only time we were allowed to scream at the kids was when they first came into the facility so that we could get their undivided attention. Many of the kids thought it was a joke coming into maximum prison. But after we got their attention, we began to educate them about peer pressure, AIDS, drugs, and prison life. After the seminar, each kid had the opportunity to write back to inform us about what they learned or didn't like about the seminar. The kids would always write how much they learned and appreciated coming to the program.

I remember the first time I went before the kids to talk about the importance of getting an education. At one point, I was messing up so much that the director told me to sit down. I couldn't go before the kids again until I convinced the director that I could perform. He taught me well because he was a very patient brother who was sincerely trying to reach those kids.

When the director allowed me to give my education presentation again before about thirty kids, he told me I did an excellent job.

Although I still made mistakes and froze during my presentation, I just played it off by going to one of the kids and asking him a question. As the kid was answering my question, I got my thoughts back on track or one of the team members would throw me a lifeline.

We had seminars on Mondays, Wednesdays, and Fridays. After all the presentations were given in a big circle, we broke into small groups so that we could get to know the kids on a more personal level. Confidentiality was very important. If something was discussed in the small group and it got out, the director would fire you from the team. He didn't play games when it came to confidentiality.

I was active in a bunch of different programs: as a teacher's aide, on the YAP team, and officiating basketball games for the rec department. I was helping the inmates organize family events. And before I knew it, a year had gone by. I didn't receive any misbehavior reports, and I only had one more year before I would go before the parole board for the second time. I was definitely looking forward to going home.

"Without the church, without religion, I would never have been here today."

—Nelson Mandela
1999

Second Parole Board Appearance (1996)

I had been in Fishkill a little over a year now. I was looking forward to going before the parole board this time. I was staying out of trouble. In my mind, I was doing everything that was expected of me, and I knew my chances of getting parole were really good.

I avoided a lot of incidents, even when some of the younger Muslims were harassing and threatening to do bodily harm to me. The younger inmates who I was working out with wanted to fight these Muslim brothers for me, but I discouraged them because I didn't want them to get into trouble.

Although I was trying to stay out of trouble, I was ready to protect myself by any means necessary, so I had to stay on point. I slept with one eye open because anyone could attack you while sleeping. When watching TV, I would stand against the wall in the back of the TV room. When I was in the yard, I was either working out or kicking it with the young ones who were in my circle. I came to the conclusion that the young Muslims were just bluffing. They were just talking to be heard because back in the day, when someone got out of line, we stepped to handle our business without any hesitation.

Several jails were in an uproar because in 1995 a new Republican governor was elected in the state of New York. Governor George Pataki built his campaign upon the violence in New York. When he came into office in January, the first thing he did in corrections was to stop violent offenders from getting work release. I had just been approved for work release under the Cuomo administration, but when Pataki took office, he eradicated work release for violent offenders. He stopped college grants so that inmates couldn't attend college.

And he made it very difficult for inmates who had committed violent crimes to get paroled. It was crazy because thirty inmates would go before the parole board and only one would get parole. The jails were in a frenzy. All those who anticipated going before the parole board were discouraged because they knew that they would be given another two years. Even the COs were panicking because the governor was laying off COs and closing down jails. The COs used to get so discouraged that they tried to get the inmates to riot so that the COs could justify their jobs. The COs would do things like tell us that the administration was going to stop the phone program, our only contact with the outside world besides receiving visits. The COs knew the inmates would go off and riot because of those telephones.

When Pataki took office, he took hope away from both inmates and COs. The only difference was that inmates had no choice but to endure all that the governor did while the COs got to go home to their families every night. Everyone who went before the parole board for a violent crime was given an additional two years no matter what the nature of the crime was. I didn't know the circumstances of the other inmates who were going before the board, but as far as I was concerned, I knew I didn't commit the crime.

I heard one story about a female, Katherine Borden, who was in Bedford Hills Correctional Facility. She was convicted of killing an armored truck guard. She was sentenced to fifteen years to life. When she went before her first parole board, she was given two additional years. She went to her second parole board appearance, and the parole commissioner who interviewed her gave her a date to go home.

When Governor Pataki found out that the parole board gave her a date to go home, he tried to stop her from going home, but it was too late. So the governor demoted the commissioner who interviewed her to a lower position. He wanted to fire the commissioner, but he didn't have the authority to do so. From that point on, all the parole commissioners were intimidated by Pataki because they didn't want to be demoted to a lower paying position. Therefore, the percentage of the violent offenders that were released went drastically down as compared to when Cuomo was in office.

I started to doubt that I was going to go home. I knew I could handle another two years, but I was concerned about my daughter. I didn't want to disappoint her again. I didn't want to break her spirit, although I didn't have the power to change anything.

The closer I came to the appearance date, the more apprehensive I became. I was on an emotional roller coaster. Honestly, I was scared to death about getting another two years. I wanted out bad. I wanted to go home. I had been incarcerated for almost seventeen years for a crime I didn't do. Didn't I deserve to go home? I didn't know what to think.

But I held on to what little hope I had. I continued working with the kids and helping inmates obtain their GED. I continued organizing the Family Day events. I was on the Inmate Liaison Committee, which represented the population to the administration. And I didn't receive any misbehavior reports in almost two years. What more could the parole board want?

All sorts of thoughts were going through my mind as I got closer to my next parole board hearing. The institution's parole officer called me down to his office to interview me regarding my institution record, my program record, my past history, and the nature of the crime I was convicted for. Every board required the institutional parole officer to interview each inmate two months prior to the actual parole board date.

When I went before the commissioners at my second parole board, I was so nervous I couldn't speak. All I could think about was two more years and this new governor. When it was time for me to speak, I kept stuttering. I don't remember how long I was in the room. I blanked out mentally.

I waited for their decision for two days, and those were the longest two days of my incarceration. I couldn't sleep, I cried, and I prayed that they let me go home. When I received the decision, I was scared to open the envelope. I walked away from the others who were also waiting for their decision and put the envelope in my pocket. Once I got away from everyone, I opened the envelope, and the first thing I saw was "Parole Denied. Next appearance 1998." My heart dropped.

Someone later told me that I was walking around in a daze. Several guys asked me why they'd given me another two years, but I didn't want to talk. The only reason why the parole board gave me another two years was because of the nature of the crime.

I was angry. How was I going to tell my daughter? I didn't have the heart. It took me months before I told her. Taneé was now about eighteen years old. She was only about thirteen months when I left her. Unbelievable!

Third and Fourth Parole Board Appearances

I spoke to my brother Joe about telling my daughter, and he wanted me to speak to her face to face. I agreed. When Joe, Jamal, Sam, and my daughter, Taneé, came to see me, the first thing my daughter said to me was "Dad, they aren't ever going to let you go."

My heart dropped when she said that. I didn't know how she knew. I couldn't say anything else because the system had stolen her faith. I didn't know what to think. Was my daughter right? Was I ever going home?

Both parole board decisions indicated that I didn't take any responsibility, and I didn't show any remorse. The parole board wanted me to admit to a murder that I hadn't committed. How could I admit to killing a fifty-nine-year-old legally blind man? I couldn't do it. According to the Bible, murder was the worst sin.

When the visit was over, my daughter was crying. When she looked back and saw me standing behind the gate, I felt so bad for her because she didn't understand the full extent of what I was going through. All she wanted was her father. She believed that I didn't commit the crime. But she didn't know when I was coming home.

I remember asking my daughter how she felt about me being out of her life. She responded that all of her friends were growing up without their fathers. I don't remember what I said, but I wasn't surprised, because it seemed to me that all the black men were incarcerated, especially during the crack era. I knew my daughter was in pain, although she tried to hide it. The pain would really come when we talked on the phone. She would sound very sad. I would ask her what was wrong, and she would say nothing was wrong. There were many times I wished I could reach through the telephone and give her a hug and tell her everything was going to be all right. I kept urging her to remain strong and telling her that she gave me strength. Indeed, she was my source of strength.

I continued doing positive things within prison. The three main places that you could find me were at the YAP office, the church, or the workout are in the yard. I was no longer a teacher's aide because I became the director of the Youth Assistance Program. When the former director was transferred to a lower classification facility, the YAP team had to select a director. One of the guys nominated me over the existing assistant director. The assistant director thought he was going to be selected automatically. He argued and fought the members by saying there wasn't going to be a vote. Things got so bad that we had to bring in the staff advisor to supervise the election. The vote was 11 to 1. The assistant director was the only one who voted against me.

After I became the director, he quit the YAP team. The only thing I changed was that everyone had the opportunity to speak with the chaperones while the small groups were in session instead of just the director and assistant director. Chaperones weren't allowed in the small groups because we encouraged the youths to talk freely.

I also stayed in the church because there was always something going on like choir rehearsals, Bible studies, and leadership classes. I used to love leading the congregational songs. Although I don't consider myself a singer, I felt I was singing up a storm. The congregation used to love it when I led those songs because they knew I was scared to death. But I wouldn't allow fear to stop me from singing.

I also was constantly working out in the yard. Working out helped me tremendously to sustain my body, mind, and soul. It helped me vent out all the negative energy that I accumulated being in that environment.

I occupied my time with these three pursuits, and time went by so fast that I was within months of my third parole board hearing. In my preparation for my appearance, I asked the superintendent for a recommendation letter, and he agreed. Once I obtained the letter, my hope of going home went up. He wrote about my being on the YAP team, my good disciplinary record, and my becoming a role model within the prison. I was impressed because I didn't know he thought of me in such a way.

But when I went before the parole board for the third time, parole denied. I was given another two years; next appearance in 2000. The reason: the severity of the crime, not taking responsibility, and not showing any remorse. The same reasons they gave at my first, second, and now third time. It was crazy because the only thing that kept going through my mind was what my daughter said: "Dad, they are never going to let you go."

I asked the pastor about admitting to the crime. He responded that I had to make that decision for myself. He also said, "Sometimes a person must humble himself to get peace of mind." I thought about that statement for many nights because there was definitely some validity to it. But again, I couldn't do it. Every time my mind would tell me to go ahead and submit, my heart wouldn't allow me to.

So when I went before the parole board for the fourth time, again I was denied parole and was given two more years. Next appearance 2002: Reason: Nature of the crime, not taking responsibility for the crime, and not showing any remorse.

Although I was hurting when I got the decision, deep down I knew I wasn't going home because I would not admit to the crime. Now I was definitely leaning toward admitting to the crime. What did it matter? Being right and telling the truth weren't getting me any justice. I grew desperate. I wanted out by any means necessary.

Therefore, I decided to admit to the crime at my fifth parole board. My hope rose a little because if the parole board wanted to hear me admit to the crime, I guess they would let me go. I spoke to my daughter about admitting to the crime, and she said it was my decision. Only she and my brother Joe knew I was going to admit to the crime at the next hearing. Well, I had two more years to think about it.

Fifth and Sixth Parole Board Appearances

Yes, I decided to admit to the crime at my fifth parole board. Although my heart was telling me not to do it, my mind became desperate wanting to go home. I was much older, and I was looking at life with a different set of glasses. I was strictly focusing on me and the parole board. It was the year 2000, and I had been in prison for over twenty years. I was trying my best to hold on and stay positive by being helpful throughout the population.

The young boys had gotten worse as far as the gangs were concerned. They were still cutting each other in the face with razors. The prison environment had gotten worse: the medical treatment, the food, the programs, every aspect of prison life. I wanted out bad. It was the only thing I was thinking about at this point. I didn't know what to do with myself. Although I was still working out, I worked out mainly by myself because the young guys I used to work out with had gone home. I tried not to get too close to anyone, because every time I got close to someone, he would leave and go home.

Time seemed to be going much slower than before. As I said, it was the year 2000, "Y2K." No one knew what was going to happen to their computers. Everyone thought that computers were going to crash. People started withdrawing their money from the banks. People were stocking up on supplies. And even all the inmates were worried about the administration's computers losing track of our prison time. Inmates throughout the state of New York were talking about shutting down the prisons. We wanted answers.

In Fishkill, word was going around that all the inmates were going to strike on a particular date. The administration got wind of this and established special investigators to look into the possible strike. The first thing the investigators did was pull all the so-called "troublemakers" together and interview them. If the investigator felt that anyone was a threat to the prison, they transferred the inmate to a maximum prison immediately.

The dorm that I was in was located in the back of the facility. When the day came to strike, we struck. But we didn't know if the other dormitories in the facility were striking or not. The inmates in my dorm didn't want to leave the building, because they were scared that if they went against the strike, they would be either stabbed or sliced across their faces. We were in the dark about the movement of the population.

The next thing I knew, a riot squad, about four sergeants and two captains, busted into our dorm and told all the inmates to return to their individual cubes. One inmate was walking too slow for one of guards, and he pushed the inmate. The inmate turned around and started swinging. The inmate punched the guard across his helmet, which hurt his hand. Before the inmate could recover, there were about four riot guards jumping on him. They made an example out of him to let us know they weren't playing games.

As that commotion was taking place, one of the riot guards that I knew told me that our dorm was the only dorm that was striking. The captain announced that if we didn't get to program within ten minutes, he would transfer all of us to a maximum facility. No one moved. Since we were in the dark about the movement of the population, and the CO had told me that our dorm was the only dorm to strike, I decided to make the first move to leave the dorm. I could feel all the inmates' eyes on my back as I walked toward the exit. When I got into the corridor, the first thing I saw was inmates walking to and from either the mess hall or various programs. I immediately went back to the dormitory and told everyone we were the only ones who were striking.

The investigators called me down to the office a few hours later. They thought I was one of the leaders of the strike, but I convinced them that I wasn't. I told them it didn't matter if the computer crashed or not because I had evidence of my time. I informed them I had parole board papers that verified my time. Also, I told them I was the director of YAP. They decided not to transfer me back to a maximum prison. I certainly didn't want to go back there because it felt like going backwards. I was trying to move forward and get out of prison.

It was now 2001. I was at the YAP office when one of the members ran in yelling that New York was being attacked. We didn't know what he was talking about until someone else came running into the office and informed us that the Twin Towers were hit by planes and that it was on the news. We all went back to our respective dormitories.

When I got back to the dormitory, the first thing I saw on TV was the first tower being hit by a plane. It was crazy because there were people jumping out of windows to escape the fire from the plane. I was looking at the TV with my month wide open because I couldn't believe what I was seeing. Then another plane hit the second tower. Some of the inmates were cheering for those who were responsible. This caused fights among the inmates because some of them had family members who worked at the World Trade Center. The COs started jumping on the inmates who were cheering for those cowards.

The jail was in an uproar. Many of the inmates went to the box because of their stupid comments. Many were sent back to maximum facility prisons because of the security of the jail. Things got so bad that the administration closed the facility for security reasons. All outside activities were suspended until further notice. We were only allowed to stay in the dormitories where we either cooked, watched TV, or stayed in our cubes.

I became really depressed. I didn't know if any of my family members had been working in the Twin Towers or not. Anytime a major incident happened in society, the administration cut all the telephones off. I never understood why the administration shut down the only communication we had with our loved ones. We were in the dormitories for three days before they opened the programs and the yard.

Prison life in Fishkill was really slow for me after 9/11. The only thing I was concerned about was the parole board. I was thinking about resigning from the YAP program because I couldn't concentrate. The guys convinced me not to resign because they felt I would wig out by thinking so much. They told me that I needed to have something to do to keep my mind off the parole board. I agreed. Sure enough, time went by faster. I was preparing for the fifth board. I really didn't have anything to prepare because I knew what I was going to say. I was going to lie, which would be difficult for me, but I felt like I had no other choice. I would admit to the murder.

At the hearing, when they asked me who did the shooting, I told them that my codefendant did the actual shooting. My codefendant was murdered in 1982. He had already told me that he and my brother were involved. They asked me why we had to kill him. The questions were getting harder for me to answer because I didn't know. So I told them that it shouldn't have happened. I believe they knew I was lying by the way the commissioner was looking at me. I kept telling them that I was sorry and that it shouldn't have happened. They thanked me and said I would get their decision within three days.

Those were the longest three days in my life. I had a fifty–fifty chance of going home. Fifty percent was good odds. In fact, I felt good about it to the point that I was telling everyone that I might be going home. But when I got the decision, once again, parole denied. Next appearance: 2004. Reason: Nature of crime and I could not stay at liberty in society. I was mad. I felt sick. I felt as if I'd sold my soul to the devil. I couldn't believe I wasn't going home after that last commissioner made me feel that, if I admitted to the crime, I would go home.

The same exact thing happened when I went before my sixth parole board appearance. I figured since the fifth parole board appearance was the first time I admitted to the crime, they wanted to see if I would admit to the crime at my sixth appearance. So I said I did it. The commissioner kept asking me, "Why did you have to kill him?" Every time I answered it shouldn't have happened, but my voice shook, and I was stuttering so badly that I stopped talking completely—shutdown. Decision: Parole denied: Next appearance: 2006. Reason: Nature of crime and I couldn't stay at liberty in society. Unbelievable!

"The cell is an ideal place to learn to know yourself, to search realistically and regularly the process of your own mind and feelings."

—Nelson Mandela
February 11, 1994

Otisville Correctional Facility

"Murray," said the dorm CO, "pack all your personal belongings and take them to the receiving room. You are going to be transferred."

Wow, I didn't expect that. I didn't have any idea which facility I was going to. I thought that maybe the transfer was related to the strike incident and that I was going back to a maximum-security prison. I prayed that wasn't the case because I didn't want to go back into a dangerous environment. I wanted to go home, and upstate wasn't in that direction. None of the COs who worked in the receiving room would tell me where the bus was going.

While the property CO was packing my property, the YAP staff advisor came down to the receiving room to see me. On the down low, he informed me that I was going to Otisville Correctional Facility, a medium-security facility. I was kind of glad I was being transferred. Going into a new environment would make the time go faster.

Otisville was only forty-five minutes from New York City. I guess I was getting closer to home after all, even though it was by going from prison to prison. The ride to Otisville was quick, about a half hour. When I saw the facility, it reminded me of a college campus. As I got closer, I noticed there were no gates separating the yard from the main population like the arrangement at Fishkill. Inmates were standing all over the facility conversing. I had never seen anything like it before. I didn't see any COs in the yard or around the compound as the bus was heading toward the receiving room.

When we got into the receiving room, within five minutes we were given our property and escorted to the dorms. I couldn't believe we weren't searched. The CO told us that the population was about thirteen hundred. The majority of the inmates in Otisville population were lifers. I asked the CO to repeat what he'd just said, and he said again, "The majority of the inmates in the Otisville population are lifers." I couldn't believe it. The environment and the layout of the facility were cool, but had I been transferred to Otisville to rot? The CO took me to Unit 21. As I walked toward it, I saw some really old faces—faces that went back to when I was at the Atlantic Avenue jail when I first got busted in 1979. Crazy!

The next day I went to the Program Committee, and they assigned me to Transitional Services. I had the same responsibilities when I was working in prerelease, except a few more programs were added. Albany had changed the name because it wasn't just about releasing inmates. There were too many inmates coming back and forth to prison at a very high rate. I believe the prison recidivism rate was about 72 percent.

It was one of the reasons why the parole board was so hard on us. Under the old prerelease program, the only things that were required by the parole board were proof of residence and a letter of reinsurance from an agency indicating they would assist you in obtaining employment. Under the new Transitional Services, you must also obtain a certificate in violence, drugs, learning how to write a resume, how to go on an interview for a job, how to dress for a job, and how to adapt in society without coming back to prison.

I didn't understand why the Program Committee assigned me to Transitional Services to assist inmates on how to adjust in society. I had been in prison for twenty-five years. How was I going to help someone stay out of jail? I could definitely teach them how to adjust to prison life without getting themselves murdered, but I certainly couldn't teach them how to stay outside. Many of the inmates I knew from the old days told me that the parole board was rejecting them repeatedly. It was true that the majority of inmates in Otisville were lifers. They also felt the same way, that they were placed at Otisville to rot in jail. My faith in the parole board was already at an all-time low, and now it was downright depressing.

Time did, in fact, go by quickly. I was now preparing for my seventh parole board appearance. I was still apprehensive about admitting to the crime, but I felt like I didn't have any other choice if I wanted go home.

When I went before the parole board on May 18, 2006, after going over the preliminaries of why I was before them, they asked me to tell them about the crime. I told them I was sorry and that it shouldn't have happened. I spoke about my accomplishments while incarcerated: I earned my high school diploma and an Associate of Arts degree from the Ulster County Community College. I earned over twenty certificates of merit, for example completing training as a teacher's aide, volunteering for Youth Assistance Program, and completing courses in parenting, nonviolent conflict resolution, and religious education. I also told them I had obtained numerous certificates of appreciation for my efforts. Finally, I told them I hadn't received any misbehavior reports in over ten years.

When I finished speaking, they asked me a few more questions that I couldn't answer. Then they asked me if I had anything else to say before they concluded the hearing. Something came over me to not leave that room without telling the truth. I was in that room for about fifteen minutes telling them how sorry I was and that the crime shouldn't have happened, but in that last minute I turned my whole testimony around and told them I didn't commit the crime.

The commissioner who was asking the questions looked at me like I was crazy. He had an expression on his face that let me know that he wasn't happy about my change in testimony. He indicated that I was in the room for about fifteen minutes telling the board how sorry I was, but at the last minute I changed my story. I told them that it didn't matter what they did to me; it was about me standing up for the truth regardless of the consequences. I felt really good about telling the truth. I felt awful the first time I admitted to the crime at the fifth parole board appearance.

Their decision was that I was once again denied parole and given another two years; next appearance 2008. Reasons: nature of the crime, and I wouldn't stay at liberty in society. I wasn't even upset when I got the decision. My prayer to God was that He would put in the commissioners' hearts to release me and let me go home. I believed that God would answer my prayer because I once again stood on the truth, and He would not approve of lies. I knew I would be all right.

FREEDOM AT LAST

Yes, I felt better about telling the truth. Something had just come over me that told me, "Don't leave this parole room without standing on the truth." I didn't care about another two years. I didn't care about the reason they were giving me two more years. The only thing that was important to me was putting everything in God's hands.

I had been praying and asking God to let me go home, even though I was telling the parole board a lie. I knew from all my studies of the Bible that God doesn't stand on lies. It was impossible for God to bless me after lying about murdering a fifty-nine-year-old legally blind man.

I also knew that things were going to be all right because God was talking to me. He was telling me to be patient. Be still. My spiritual life went to another level. I remember when I got back from the parole board, I told everyone the parole board was going to give me two years. But it didn't matter at that point because I knew God had my back.

Also, I made a conscious decision not to allow anyone to steal my joy. I was feeling blessed. Some of the inmates thought I was on a spiritual high. The population started calling me "Happy Herb." They didn't understand why I was so happy being incarcerated for over twenty-seven years.

I started reflecting on the less fortunate: inmates who went blind while incarcerated, inmates rolling around the facility on dollies because they didn't have any legs, inmates who couldn't talk, or the many inmates who were dying because of cancer or AIDS. I said to myself that if God had placed me in this situation, He must have a purpose.

Three months after my seventh parole board appearance, I received a letter from Mr. Feder, my old lawyer who represented me at my second trial. It was by the grace of God that Mr. Feder was contacting me because I hadn't heard from him in over twenty years. I couldn't believe what the letter said. He indicated that he was down in his basement looking through his files, and he thought about me. He looked me up in the computer to see if he could find a civilian address for me. He said he was shocked to find out that I was still incarcerated. The letter also mentioned that after the verdict was rendered, the judge told him that had I had a nonjury trial, he would have acquitted me. He ended the letter saying that he would do everything in his power to get me out of prison.

I was so happy that I started crying. I couldn't believe what he said about the judge. So even the judge thought that the evidence was insufficient to support a conviction. Why didn't he set aside the verdict? Didn't he have the power to do so? Didn't he have the power to dismiss the indictment before he gave the case to the jury because the evidence was insufficient? In fact, Mr. Feder argued on appeal that the evidence was so incredible that it didn't support guilty beyond a reasonable doubt as the law required. Now, after I'd served an additional fourteen years on top of the fifteen years to life that the trial judge sentenced me to, here he was saying that the evidence was insufficient. Why hadn't Mr. Feder, the prosecutor, or the judge told me this years ago?

I was angry. But on the other hand, I was saying, "Thank You, Jesus." The reason they didn't mention it before was not important to me. What was important was that they were willing to help me get out now. I knew God had sent me an angel. I asked Mr. Feder if he could obtain a letter from the trial judge. Not only did I receive a letter from Mr. Feder telling me that a second-look program had taken my case, but also he enclosed the letter from the trial judge. I was so happy, I couldn't stop smiling. I told everyone I knew and even strangers. I knew God was making a statement. It was only in the name of Jesus Christ that

His light was shining on me. My hope went sky-high, not just hoping to go home but recognizing that God is good.

The next letter I received was from the Second Look Program, a clinic at the Brooklyn Law School. Professor William E. Hellerstein was the director, and Professor Andrew E. Abraham was the assistant director. The letter said, "The clinic (made up of law students) investigates claims of innocence by inmates in New York State's correctional facilities who have exhausted their regular avenues of appeal." It also said, out of over 4000 requests for assistance, they had selected twelve cases, and mine was one of the twelve. It also noted that Mr. Feder had come to their office, shocked that I was still imprisoned, and sought the clinic's assistance.

As I was reading the letter, I must have stopped reading it at least twenty times and screamed, "Thank You, Jesus." I read that letter a hundred times the day I received it. A few months later, I received another letter from the law school, indicating that Professor Hellerstein and three law students were coming to Otisville to visit me. They came to see me right before my eighth parole board appearance. They wanted to assess what kind of individual I was and discuss the strategy they wanted to use for getting me out of prison. They suggested two approaches: either appealing to the courts or appealing to the parole board. The court was a long process and could take a very long time, but I was within months of my eighth parole board. I agreed that the process should be to appeal to the parole board.

When I went before my eighth parole board, waiting to go into the room was the longest wait in my life. I was so nervous. Every time I went to the parole board, they would call the inmates by alphabetical order according to their last name. When it was my turn to go into the room, they skipped my name. I was the very last one to go into the room. I didn't know what to think. Although I felt good and confident that I was going home, I had been disappointed so many times before that I still had a little doubt.

I was finally called into the room. After going over the preliminaries of why I was there, the commissioner said, "Wow! A lot of people believe in your innocence." She also asked, "Why didn't they come forward a long time ago?" I knew I was going home because they'd never asked me this line of questions before, especially when it came to my innocence. The commissioner kept saying, "Wow." She couldn't believe I had done twenty-nine years for a crime that I didn't commit.

Again, I had to wait three long days to receive the board's decision. When I received the letter, the first thing that caught my attention was that the envelope wasn't as heavy as the previous decisions' envelopes, which were always full of appeal papers. There wasn't any appeal paper in this envelope. Parole granted. Date to be released: on or before May 8, 2008.

I couldn't believe it! I was going home at last. Thank You, Jesus! Words couldn't describe my happiness. My daughter at first didn't believe me when I told her I was coming home, even though she knew I had so many people pushing for my release. I was the happiest person alive when I walked out of Otisville Correctional Facility eight days later, after being in prison for twenty-nine years. Wow!

"I am absolutely excited to be out."

—Nelson Mandela
1990

Welcome Home

My date to go home was May 8, 2008. I had already done my homework about obtaining a letter from an agency that would assist me in gaining employment and a place to live when I got out. I thought about asking my daughter if I could live with her, but I didn't want to impose. Also, I felt as a man that I needed to stand on my own two feet.

The day before I was released, the institution's parole officer called me down to explain parole stipulations. He informed me that I must report to the outside parole officer within twenty-four hours. I signed the stipulations paperwork. He then said, "Good luck."

I couldn't sleep at all. I stood up all night waiting for daylight. The CO had to take me to the state shop to get my parole clothes. It was after 10:00 a.m., and the CO still didn't come for me. I kept asking the dorm CO to call Administration, but the CO kept telling me that someone was coming. I was getting mad because usually the inmates who were scheduled to go home would be out of the facility by 10:00 a.m.

Finally a sergeant came to the dorm, and I asked him to call Administration. He did and told me that someone was on his way to get me. I said to myself, if I could do twenty-nine years, I certainly could wait another few hours.

The CO finally came and took me to the state shop. From the state shop I went to the administration building to be fingerprinted and photographed for an identification card. I was given forty dollars and a bus ticket to New York City. The CO took me to a bus terminal, told me good luck, and drove off.

I was scared to death. I didn't know which direction to walk, so I went along with the crowd. Once I got on the bus, I handed my ticket to the bus driver, who told me that the ticket had expired. I couldn't believe the facility had given me an expired bus ticket! I had to use some of the forty dollars to get back to the city. Anyway, I made sure that I sat close to the window so I could see the new world without having on handcuffs, smiling from ear to ear.

I was thinking about the forty dollars and how it was a trap for many individuals who got caught up in the revolving door into and out of prison. After doing twenty-nine years, how in the world was a grown man going to get started in life with forty dollars? But I understood the lesson. I must not be a victim. I needed a job. I needed money—legal money, that is. I made a decision right there on the bus to New York City that I would find a job. I had been hustling jobs since I was twelve years old. I knew how to get a job even after twenty-nine years off the street.

I couldn't believe I was in New York City's Port Authority and then Times Square. I was waiting on my daughter. We had agreed on the time to meet according to the bus arrival schedule, but I had waited about an hour and still didn't see her. I decided to try to contact her, so I went downstairs and tried calling her on the telephone. When I inserted the quarter into the telephone, the coin kept coming back down the slot. I went to the next phone and it did the same thing. I thought the telephones were out of order. I asked someone to assist me in using the telephone, but she didn't want to give me any assistance. So I stood there not knowing what to do.

I started to go outside, but an ex-inmate came over to me and to welcome me home. He recognized the prison outfit. I asked him if he could help me contact my daughter. I told him about my attempt in calling her, but I told him all the phones were broken. He took me over to the phones, I gave him the number, and the next thing I knew I was talking to my daughter on the phone. I thanked him, and he wished me good luck.

The facility had given Taneé the wrong arrival gate for the bus. But she was just on the other side of the terminal. I couldn't believe I didn't know how to use the telephone. Before I went to prison, you would insert the coin into the slot and dial the number. But, when the ex-inmate made the call, he dialed the number and then inserted the coin when the operator ordered him to do so. I realized that I had a lot to learn.

Wow! My daughter finally came, and I was surprised that she brought my granddaughter Brenea and Jackie with her. It was the most beautiful sight in the world. We were all hugging and laughing and hugging some more. Words can't describe how I felt. I thanked God in silence. God is so good! Hallelujah!

When I got on the A train, I felt like I was on the Cyclone. I hadn't gone that fast in years. They were laughing at me when I was telling them how I felt.

I had to report to the parole office in downtown Brooklyn. When I got to the office, I was assigned to Ms. Glover. While I waiting for her to call me into her office, I asked some of the guys there if they had Ms. Glover. I was hoping that I wouldn't get a nasty parole officer. I had heard many stories about parole officers busting guys for missing their curfew.

Ms. Glover finally called me into her office, and I knew right away that God had blessed me again. She was decent. She went over the parole stipulations with me. She told me my curfew was 9:00 p.m. and that I must report to her once a week. She also informed me that she would be giving me urine tests. Of course, she didn't tell me when.

After I left her office, they took me to a Redemption Center on Herkimer Street in Brooklyn, where I would be living. After putting my clothes away, I told them I was going out with my family and I would be back by 9:00 p.m. Taneé and Jackie took me to a nice restaurant. The food was definitely different from prison food. As I was eating, I made a mental note that I must get used to the food. I was having a good time.

I was smiling so much, my jaws started hurting. We went to Taneé's house after we ate and we met a few more of my family members. I had never been hugged so many times within one day. I was definitely feeling the love. There were so many people at my daughter's house that it was only standing room. We partied until about 3:00 a.m. I was informed that the official welcome home party was going to place next week at my niece Renee's house.

During the first week I really didn't do anything but hang out and see a lot of old faces. Many people were surprised when they saw me because they thought I was dead. One person thought I'd been murdered in prison. The official welcome home party was on a Saturday, and people came from all over: My brother Joe came from Georgia, my sister Carolyn and my niece Lynette came in from Maryland, and the majority of my family came from New Jersey. I had a wonderful time. It was definitely a time I will never forget.

The Job Search

The welcome home party and seeing a lot of familiar faces was a beautiful thing, especially seeing my brother, who had supported me during the last twenty-nine years. But it was time for me to find a job.

Many were telling me that I should relax for about a month before I started to look for a job. Of course, I didn't agree because I was already twenty-nine years behind. I needed to get into the grind as soon as possible. One thing I wasn't going to do was accept a program. I'd been programming the whole time I was incarcerated.

The next day, after having the most beautiful time of my life, I went down to the welfare office and applied for public assistance, which was required by the Redemption Center, the place where I was staying. Welfare gave the Redemption Center $215 a month. They wanted my food stamps, but it wasn't part of the deal, so I declined giving them the food stamps. The only thing that was required was the $215. It may not seem a lot, but when you have ten individuals sleeping in one room and all of us were giving the Center $215, it was a lot of money. That's $2150 a month the Center was getting. Also, the Center wanted $10 from each person to use the kitchen and to watch TV. When I wrote the Redemption Center to request assistance, they informed me that I must apply for public assistance in order for them to get paid, but they didn't mention anything about an additional $20 to use the appliances.

Anyway, when I went to see Ms. Glover, she informed me about the Center for Equal Opportunity program (CEO). She highly recommended that I go there to obtain employment. I went to CEO as soon as I left the parole officer. When I got there, I spoke to a lady named Ms. Gwen, who told me that CEO didn't accept individuals who were on parole for murder. I told her my story and I showed her the judge's letter and the letter from Mr. Feder. After she read the letters, she said, "Wow." I asked her could I speak to her supervisor. I spoke to Ms. Sandy, the assistant director of CEO. She also read the letters and told Ms. Gwen to allow me to go through their orientation class. I was told to start orientation the following Monday. I was glad.

Ms. Gwen explained that I would start as a part-time worker. I was told I would be assigned to work sites and I would be making minimum wage. They gave each of us a workbook and told us that we must have the supervisor from each site sign the book upon our arrival at the site. The work sites were designed to develop work ethics: being responsible, being on time for work, getting along with co-workers and supervisors, and taking orders well. CEO didn't want to jeopardize its reputation on an individual who really didn't want to work. Therefore, before they assigned, recommended, or sent you on an interview, they wanted to know if you were a good candidate for a permanent job.

The guy who taught the class was good. His spiel had us participating, and time went by fast. Soon the class was over, and I would start work Monday. I couldn't believe I'd landed a job within two weeks after being out of prison. God is good.

When I told the director of the Redemption Center, he told me I had to give him another $20 every week because I had a part-time job. I couldn't believe this guy was asking for another $20 a week. He was definitely trying to take advantage of us. Where was I getting $80 from to give him? I told him that I would give him nothing. Therefore, he didn't allow me to use the kitchen or go into the TV room. I didn't care because I was determined to save all the money I could.

When I started working, I was getting $42 a day. I deposited the check into the bank every time I got paid. I was determined to do everything I needed to do to get on my feet. But every time I came into contact with more money, the Redemption Center wanted some of it. I became so frustrated with their greed that I had to get out of there. Many of the guys also got frustrated and left before me. I was trying to hang in there until I saved up enough money so that I could get a room, but the exploitation became so unbearable that I had to leave. I did something that I didn't want to do: I went to live with my daughter. Although I knew she would accept me without any hesitation, I stayed at the Redemption Center for about three months before I asked her if I could stay with her until I saved enough money to get a room. She accepted me without any problems. I love my baby girl. I knew she would have my back.

"One of the most difficult things is not to change society, but to change yourself."

—Nelson Mandela
February 10, 2000

The Physical Transition

Jessica, my job developer at CEO, called me into her office and asked whether I wanted to go on a job interview at the Times Square Alliance. She informed me that the job was part time, but I could be hired as a full-time worker. She indicated that the job consisted of cleaning the streets of Times Square. She also said that when I went full-time, they would give me all the benefits that the average job had. I felt good because I'd been with CEO for only about three months before I was invited to interview for a job. She told me she would be with me during the interview.

When it was time for me and two other CEO workers to be interviewed at the Times Square Alliance, I was scared because of my circumstances of being on parole for murder. I knew many frowned on individuals who were on parole for murder, but Jessica kept telling me to relax. I tried to relax, but I was nervous. When we got to the office of the Alliance, the first person they called into the office was a man named Darryl. It seemed that he was in there for about a half-hour. The longer he was in the office, the more apprehensive I became about telling my story. When Darryl came out of the office, he was grinning from ear to ear; they'd given him a job.

They called me next. When I went into the office, there was the vice president of Times Square Alliance, Bob Esposito; the Director of Sanitation, Joe Costarella; and Jessica, who sat right by my side. She gave them my resume. The first question the vice president asked me was why I was incarcerated. I explained the reason why I was incarcerated, and I showed him the letters from the judge and my lawyer. He also asked me what I did while I was incarcerated.

Jessica jumped in to give me support. She told them about my work performance while being at CEO. She spoke very highly of me. After Jessica finished speaking, the vice president told me to have a seat outside. I knew for sure that I wasn't going to get the job because they told Darryl right there that he was hired. When I went back into the office, Jessica was smiling when I looked at her. The vice president told me that he was going to give me a chance and he hoped that I wouldn't disappoint him. I was smiling from ear to ear when he told me that. Jessica congratulated me and told me I would do all right. I really appreciated Jessica because she went out of her way to make sure I had my resume intact. All three of us went back to the offices of CEO with big smiles on our faces. We were to start working for the Times Square Alliance the following Monday.

I felt good about the whole thing. I knew God had blessed me once again. I couldn't wait. I knew it was a great opportunity for me, because Jessica kept telling both of us that once we were hired, we would have benefits. When I got to the sanitation office, located on 39th Street between Eight and Ninth Avenues, Joe, the director, gave me a work schedule from 5:30 a.m. to 1:30 p.m. on Thursdays, Fridays, and Saturdays. My off days were on Sunday through Wednesday. It was a tight schedule, but I knew I needed a steady job. I didn't care if I had to get up 4:00 a.m.

As we were sitting waiting for roll call, I observed my surroundings. I noticed that the majority of the workers were Hispanics and blacks. I think there were about thirty of us sitting there waiting for our assignments for the day. I was assigned to a supervisor to teach me the routes throughout Times Square. The day went by quickly.

When I got off from work, the president of the Redemption Center wanted to speak to me. He wanted me to become the building manager, which entailed keeping the house in order. He said that I would be responsible for making sure that everyone met his curfew.

I decided to take him up on his offer. I didn't enforce the curfew law too well because I understood. Otherwise, the only thing I required from anyone who stayed out after curfew was that he had to call me. I also told them that if their parole officer came to the house, I wouldn't be responsible. By 9:00 p.m. I was in bed, because I had to get up at 4:00 a.m. to go to work. Many times I didn't know if the guys were in the house or not. I felt the guys were already under pressure from their parole officer, so why should I add to the pressure?

Also, I stayed out past my curfew myself. In fact, about three months after I took the building manager position, I stayed out all night. On my way back to the Redemption Center, I felt something was wrong with my parole officer. I couldn't put my finger on it, but I knew something was wrong. Instead of going back to the Redemption Center, I proceeded to my parole officer's office. As soon as she called me into her office, I knew that she was aware that I had stayed out all night. I sat down and told her I was out all night because I went to a party and it was too late for me to go to the Redemption Center. She told me she knew because the president of the Redemption Center had called her.

I was mad because I was working for this fool as the building manager, and he had the audacity to call my parole officer and try to get me in trouble? This dude did about eighteen years in prison himself. Because he wanted some recognition from the parole people, he went out of his way to try to get the guys violated. Many of the guys wanted to jump on him, but they knew he would tell. No one liked this guy because not only did he do eighteen years in prison, but he knew better than to tell on someone. He knew that in prison, he would have been murdered.

After he told my parole officer I was out all night, I wanted out of the Redemption Center. Therefore, I decided to something I didn't want to do. I asked my daughter if I could stay with her and my granddaughter. Of course, she accepted me with open arms.

Being in my daughter's household gave me the opportunity to bond with her and my granddaughter. When I got there, my granddaughter was so happy because she knew I would take her out with me. She definitely had me wrapped around her finger, although I used to deny it. I used to love spoiling her. I used to take her and her cousin swimming. I remember the first time I took her swimming. She was scared to go into the water until I got in first. I really appreciated the bonding because although I knew my granddaughter when I was incarcerated, there wasn't any true relationship between us because I didn't see her that much. Being incarcerated stole my relationship not only with my daughter but also with my granddaughter. It's a shame what the system did to me!

I remember one day a few of the sanitation guys were arguing about a statement made regarding the company giving us a second chance. I asked them was there something wrong with someone giving us a second chance? Second chance means you were once down and out and that you needed help to stand again. I told them I knew I was given a second chance. God was ordering my footsteps and placing people in my path so that they could do His will by helping me stand tall. Therefore, I was definitely given another chance and was grateful that the Alliance had given me a job. Furthermore, I felt that if someone was either coming home from being incarcerated or recovering from a drug addiction or alcoholism, he should definitely get a second chance.

I noticed many times when we were sitting in the sanitation office waiting to be assigned our duties for the day, there was a lot of arguing among the workers. After a while, I found myself engaging in those arguments. It was easy for me to get involved in those arguments because in prison we argued all day just to pass the time. I came to the realization that although we were blessed in many ways, our mentality from the past wouldn't allow us to recognize our blessings.

After about three months, I was hired as a full-time worker. I was told to go to see the vice president. When I got to his office, he told me that he heard that I was doing a good job and that I was in his office to be hired full-time. I was smiling from ear to ear because I remembered his statement when I was first hired: "I hope you don't disappoint me." I was in his office about an hour speaking to him. He wanted to know more about my situation. After I explained it to him, he told me that if I needed anything or needed to talk, I shouldn't hesitate to come and see him. We shook hands, and I left.

Once again, God had blessed me because I was informed that very few were hired within that short a time. When I got back to the sanitation office, everyone congratulated me. After I was hired full time, I was called to the eighth floor to see Hollis in the human resources department. He helped me establish my 403(b) plan and medical insurance, and he gave me all the rules and regulations that governed the Times Square Alliance.

After three months of being a full-time employee, I received a telephone call from Ms. Wilson, a counseling aide who taught a certification class at Otisville Correctional Facility. She knew an individual who was being hit at the parole board continually and she wanted to help him by going to the *New York Times*. She knew a reporter who worked at the New York Times building on 43rd Street between Seventh and Eighth Avenues. Apparently, she remembered my parole story and told the reporter. When she contacted me to tell me that a reporter wanted to speak with me regarding my experience with the parole board, I was very surprised. In fact, I was in shock, but in a good way because I would have another outlet to tell my story. She was a very sweet woman, very soft spoken. God was blessing me again.

A few days later, Jackie and I went to the New York Times building. We met a reporter named Tremaine Lee. He explained to me that he wanted a story about how the New York State Parole Division was continually giving individuals two additional years for the same reason. He asked for my permission to tell my story of doing twenty-nine years for a murder I didn't commit. He recorded everything I told him. A few days later, he asked to come by my house to do the interview with a camera crew. He then asked if he could record me while I was working.

I needed to get permission from my boss. Luckily, my boss agreed, and I was happy about the whole thing because I was getting some exposure.

When Tremaine and the camera guy came to my house, they interviewed me and my daughter. They had all these lights and pinned a small microphone on the collar of my sweater. I was scared to death because I didn't know what to expect. They made me as comfortable as they could, but it didn't help because I was too scared. When the interview started, I kept telling myself to relax and take my time when talking because when I become nervous, I have a tendency to start stuttering.

The reporter also interviewed my daughter. He was asking her questions like how she felt growing up without a father and how she felt about her father being home after so many years. I remember my daughter telling the reporter that it gave her the opportunity to understand herself better by having me around.

After the interview, we drove to my job. I already knew what route I was working that day because my boss wanted me on lower Broadway so that I could be close to the administration building and the director could keep an eye on me. When it was all over, I felt good about the interview. Tremaine kept telling me that I did very good job and that he would make my story come alive.

The story aired on June 6, 2010, under the title "The Innocent Prisoner's Dilemma." New York One News, a local cable news network, picked it up and showed it. In fact, it was the most watched video. People came up to me to say that they'd just seen me on TV. I didn't get a chance to see the video when it was aired, but my story was out nevertheless, which was enough to make me smile.

THE MENTAL TRANSITION

Physically I was making a smooth transition as far as standing tall and doing what I needed to do. I obtained a full-time job, my story was publicized, and I was now living with Jackie, the mother of my daughter. I was feeling very good about myself. I also went to spend a week in Georgia at the home of my favorite brother, Joe, who took care of me during my entire incarceration. I established credit with help from Chase Bank, who lent me a thousand dollars. Of course, the bank froze a thousand dollars out of my savings for collateral.

I obtained my passport because my family was going on a family cruise. I spoke to my parole officer about me going out of the country. I was seeing a different parole officer from when I first came home because I was no longer living with my daughter in Brooklyn. My old parole officer had transferred to Manhattan. When I told my parole officer that I needed my passport to go on a cruise, he didn't have a problem with it because he told me I was doing well. But since I was requesting to go out of the country, he informed me that he had to get the approval of his supervisor. I was in his office for about forty minutes waiting for him to return from speaking to his supervisor. When he finally came back, he had a frown on his face and told me his supervisor had denied my request. I was angry and told him I was going to appeal his supervisor's denial. I also wanted him to understand that I wasn't complaining about him. He understood.

I got in contact with my lawyer and now friend, Mr. Feder. I explained the situation to him. He told me to forward all the information regarding the cruise. Two weeks later, my parole officer called me to say that the regional supervisor wanted to speak with me. When I got to the parole office, everyone was talking about why I wanted to go out of the country. I was shocked that Mr. Feder had taken care of the matter in such a short time. The regional supervisor told me that he would allow me to go on the cruise and that he would give me a letter indicating that the parole office was giving me permission to go on a cruise, just in case I was stopped by Customs.

In 2010, I went to Mexico, Grand Turk, Honduras, and the Bahamas. In 2011, not only did I go to Mexico, Belize, and Jamaica, but I was also allowed to be taken off lifetime parole. Therefore, I didn't need any permission when I went on the second cruise.

The most memorable part was spending time with my little brother Joe. At first, we didn't know he was coming on the cruise until we saw him on the ship. It was definitely a surprise. We had a ball. One week after that cruise, my brother, my hero, my rock, passed away. It was crazy because there wasn't any indication that he was sick when we were on the cruise. Just one week later, he was dead. I will never forget my brother because he had such a big heart. He was funny. He was smart. He was concerned about everyone, and he didn't refuse to help anyone. He was a big part of my life, and I will miss him forever.

Even though I had accomplished a lot within three years, I still had problems dealing with things mentally. I went on handling things as though I was still in prison. I took everything personally. I was still angry and didn't have a handle on my emotions. I was pushy and argumentative. As a result, Jackie and I broke up. I shouldn't ever have moved in with her because mentally I wasn't ready. I had just come out of an environment where I was locked down for twenty-nine years, and being controlled by someone else wasn't a good thing. Coming home and getting into a relationship was like giving up my freedom again. I needed to find my own way as opposed to being led or controlled by someone else. I wasn't ready for anything but learning how to survive in this new world without anyone holding my hand.

I made a lot of emotional mistakes because of my hardheadedness. I was on an emotional roller coaster trying to understand how things had changed. It was my assistant director at the Alliance, Rick, who took a personal interest in me. He would talk to me. He would always tell me to step back and see the bigger picture because I was so used to dealing with small things in prison. I started doing better and found myself handling things differently. Although I was still upset, I was not getting into arguments like before.

When a spot opened up on the 6:00 p.m. to 2:00 a.m. shift, Rick asked me if I wanted the position. He said it would be better for me to change my shift because I could get away from some of the workers that had caused me to be very emotional. It was definitely a blessing because my attitude started changing. I started to really appreciate life in such a way that I kept a smile on my face. People were asking me why was I so happy. I told them, God is good.

Working on Duffy Square in Times Square gave me the opportunity to interact with people from all over the world. The guys—Hargrove, our squad leader; Tyrone, Berberena, and myself—were working on Duffy Square from 2:00 p.m. until 1:30 a.m. Hargrove made sure that all the work was done. He made sure we worked in harmony. He didn't tolerate arguing. It was definitely a smooth-running shift, and it helped me with my attitude. These people made me realize that I had come from an environment totally different from this one.

A few months later, Rick called me and asked me did I have black jeans. I told him of course I had black jeans. He told me that during New Year's Eve I would be working in the Visitor Center. He told me they were going to convert the Visitor Center into a green room. All the entertainers who were going to perform during the night would be inside the green room until they were called to the stage. I had the opportunity to meet Jennifer Lopez, Lady Gaga, Justin Bieber, and many more world-renowned entertainers.

After I'd worked in the green room for New Year's Eve, a position opened up in the Visitor Center. Rick called me into his office and asked me if I wanted the position. I asked him, "Are you kidding?" I definitely wanted the position; it meant more money. Rick sent me over to speak with Tyree, the supervisor of the Visitor Center. Tyree informed me that I was highly recommended because I had done such a good job during the New Year's Eve bash. He hired me and told me to start the following day. I couldn't believe how God blessed me with a better position and making more money in such a short time. I had been working for the Alliance for only three years.

The Visitor Center was a place where tourists came to relax, obtain information, purchase tickets for Broadway shows and for sightseeing tour buses, and see the crystal Centennial New Year's Eve Ball. Tourists even got to experience a New Year's Eve countdown every twenty minutes. Tourists also had the opportunity to write their wishes on confetti and post them on the "Hopes and Dreams" wall. Those wishes become part of the ceremony the following New Year's Eve when the confetti is released.

Working in Times Square during the New Year's Eve bash is the best time of the year for me because thousands of people come from all over the world to celebrate the New Year. The celebration reminds me that I came from a totally different environment. I realize how blessed I am. Statistics say that I wasn't supposed to survive, but here I am in the midst of enjoyment, happiness, love, hugs, and laugher.

Working in the Visitor Center also gave me the opportunity to meet new people, especially from central staff at the Alliance. I went to Tim Tompkins, the president of the Alliance, to ask for a recommendation letter to present to the parole administration when I was up for release from parole. He didn't hesitate to write that letter. When I gave the letter to my parole officer to submit on my behalf, she told me that the letter was a very good recommendation. As I said before, I was granted to be off lifetime parole. Many other parolees were surprised that I was off parole because every time they were up for release, it was denied.

In my opinion, I think that letter from Tim was the main factor in my being taken off parole.

Ms. Deborah Cook was the director of Human Resources. One of her responsibilities was preparing the company's newsletter. I remember sitting in her office when I saw the *Neon News* newsletter on her desk, and I asked her if I could write an article for the newsletter. She told me of course. In my first article I wrote about how the sanitation department did such a good job in making sure that the area was clean before the trucks came in with the equipment to set up for an event.

I've been writing for the company newsletter for almost two years now and I love every moment of it because everything I write about relates to me in one way or another. In fact, writing in the newsletter motivated me to write this book. Even though my niece, Lynette, tried to motivate me to write a book way before I started writing in the newsletter, it was Ms. Cook who pushed me in writing the book after I told her my story. I asked her if she could edit my book because she was doing such a wonderful job in editing all my articles for the newsletter. I am really happy that she accepted my request because I don't think this book would have happened without her.

In addition to her, other people who work in the marketing department have played a very important part in my mental transition—people like Gary, who became the vice president of marketing and had the confidence in me to allow me to work with the marketing team for their special events. For example, for an event called "Broadway on Broadway," where all the Broadway shows preview their performance for free in Times Square, Gary had me working in the location where all entertainers practice before going on stage to perform. I loved it because it gave me the opportunity to meet all the performers. He once told me that I had the personality for interacting with the performers.

Also there is Belle, who always has a smile on her face and steadily asked me how was the book was coming along. Ruben is a really cool individual, and I learned a lot from him through the many conversations we shared. Jenny is usually my direct contact whenever I work for marketing on special events. She always encourages me by saying, "You got this, Mr. Murray." She tells me with a big smile on her face to contact her anytime if I need her. She has more confidence in me than I have in myself. She was the one who gave me my first all-access pass, which gave me the mobility to move around. She is a class act.

Damian is responsible for taking care of many things. His primary responsibility is taking care of the plazas in Time Square. He used to work for Madison Square Garden as their productions manager. He is a man of many trades. I consider him the "Jack of all trades" because he is so knowledgeable about everything.

Tom, the senior vice president of operations at the Times Square Alliance and a retired inspector for the New York Police Department, is a down-to-earth person. He works harder than any sanitation worker by a long shot. Once when I saw him with a broom and dustpan, I tried to take them away from him, and he told me he got it. One time I asked Tom for overtime because they were remodeling offices on the eighth floor. He wanted me to work with him to throw out and move desks. Tom was working harder than I was, and I consider myself a hardworking individual.

I have learned a lot from him by just observing him. He represents strength, control, and leadership. He always has a look of concentration on his face because he is either talking, texting, or looking down reading an e-mail on his phone. He is always in some form of communication with someone. I used to hear him often telling people who were in decision-making positions to "Make your decision," because I gather that if he had to make the decision for you, he didn't need you in that position.

Dafina works for finance. She is cool people because whatever is on her mind, she expresses it, regardless of how it might come out. She is an outspoken lady who doesn't care about who likes her or not.

I had a very interesting conversation with Tim's executive assistant, Robyn. I was telling her my story and told her that God put me through that situation for a reason. She told me that God didn't put me through anything. She also stated that although the devil put us through bad situations, God and His mercy help us out of those situations. It was something I had to consider. I started thinking why would God, my Father, put me through a horrible situation where I could have lost my life? I'm not questioning my spirituality or my faith in God; I just needed to understand my relationship with God and why I was placed in my situation.

In any event, I thank God for His mercy and I will always praise Him, glorify Him, and honor Him because without Him I wouldn't be standing tall thus far. Two years ago my name was drawn out of a raffle for low-income housing on 42st Street and Tenth Avenue. I was kind of intimidated to go to Tim and ask him for a recommendation letter to the management company because I had already received a letter for the parole board. I spoke to Robyn about my fear, and she told me that I shouldn't be intimidated, because if Tim can help someone, he will. However, I didn't want to abuse the privilege of going to him every time I needed help. Nevertheless, Robyn took it upon herself to represent me. She went to Tim and explained the circumstances. Sure enough, Tim was more than willing to write me the recommendation letter. I appreciate Robyn for all her assistance.

Sherry is the Director of Public Art, and she has been working for the Alliance for over a year. Since she came aboard, she definitely has made an impact at the Alliance with her creative mind. I was thinking about a design for my book. I had an idea of what I wanted, but I didn't have a clue how I was going about the design. A light went off in my head! What was I thinking about? Sherry! Why was I looking for someone to help design my book cover when I had the perfect person right under my nose?

I went to Sherry and asked if she would assist me in designing my book cover. She was more than happy to do so. In fact, her creative mind started working right there as I was requesting her assistance. She started showing me all kinds of designs, but I didn't see anything that fit my ideal book cover. Then I told her she had full control over designing the book cover. She started smiling and said, "At least someone believes in me." I started smiling.

Sam, from the communications department, has become my buddy from the time he started working at the Alliance. He graduated from Yale. Sam is a Knicks fanatic. One day, he spoke to me about a team he was on at the YMCA on 92nd Street. One day he asked me if I could coach his basketball team. I was more than willing to coach his team because when I was incarcerated I refereed or coached many games.

A few weeks after I spoke to him, I was scheduled to coach the team on a Sunday. When I got to the Y, Sam was waiting for me outside so he could escort me into the building. The team was scheduled to play their last game. While waiting, I decided to play Sam, one-on-one, so that he could be warmed up when the game started. He beat me, but he didn't know I let him win so his confidence would be high for the game.

When the game started, the team was totally out of control. They were just running up and down the court without setting up a play. They, of course, lost the game, but I had fun nonetheless. I was thinking about joining the team because they could use some leadership on the court. Also, I could help out on the board getting rebounds and playing defense. I'm looking forward to playing because I haven't played in years.

Nikki, a public safety officer, always engages me in some deep conversations. She is funny, and at the same time she can get really serious. I've learned a lot from her.

There are many others who contributed to my mental transition. My brother-in-law, Terry, is always there for me. I will always be indebted to him and rest of the people who have supported me one way or another.

One day I got the opportunity to speak to Nelson Mandela's grandsons. The Times Square Alliance arts program sponsored an event that featured some of Nelson Mandela's words. The title of the event was "The Power of Words." Everyone was invited to attend at midnight. Mr. Mandela's grandsons were, of course, the highlight of the event. I spoke to them, and I think I must have been a little talkative because Sherry had to pull me aside. It was definitely a beautiful experience and a great opportunity.

God has been good to me thus far. He has blessed me in many ways since I've been home. I believe the most important aspect of my mental transition has been surrounding myself with positive people. I remember when I was teaching at the transitional service program at Otisville Correctional Facility, and I used to tell the guys who were going home that they must surround themselves with positive people. I also told them that it didn't matter where they went in the world; if their attitudes weren't positive, they were going have a very difficult time in making the transition back into society.

May 2014 marks six years since my release. The physical and mental transition is an ongoing process until the day I die. In the meantime, I'm going to enjoy the rest of my life to the fullest. I refuse to allow anyone or anything to steal my joy. That doesn't mean I don't get upset, but life is too good not to enjoy it to the best of my ability. God is so good because if not for His keeping me during this ordeal, I could have been dead many years ago. I'm truly grateful. Thank You Jesus!